Victorian

ELEGANCE

Lezette Thomason

That Patchwork Place®

CREDITS

Editor-in-Chief **KERRY I. HOFFMAN**
Managing Editor **JUDY PETRY**
Technical Editor **MELISSA A. LOWE**
Copy Editor **LIZ MCGEHEE**
Proofreader **MELISSA RIESLAND**
Illustrator **LAUREL STRAND**
Illustration Assistant **DANI RITCHARDSON**
Photographer **BRENT KANE**
Text and Cover Designer **AMY SHAYNE**
Production Assistant **CLAUDIA L'HEUREUX**

The publishing team would like to thank the many people who graciously loaned us the heirlooms featured in this book: Mary W. Atkins, Cheryl Brown, Stephanie Cisakowski, Monica Doramus, Kay Green, Julie Ketter, Judy Petry, Katie Roe, Amy Shayne, Marion Shelton, and Barbara Weiland. Special thanks to Stephanie Cisakowski and Barbara Weiland for sharing their lovely homes.

MISSION STATEMENT

WE ARE DEDICATED TO PROVIDING QUALITY PRODUCTS AND SERVICES THAT INSPIRE CREATIVITY.

WE WORK TOGETHER TO ENRICH THE LIVES WE TOUCH.

That Patchwork Place is a financially responsible ESOP company.

Victorian Elegance
© 1996 by Lezette Thomason
That Patchwork Place, Inc., PO Box 118
Bothell, WA 98041-0118 USA

Printed in the United States of America
01 00 99 98 97 96   6 5 4 3 2 1

Library of Congress Cataloging-in-Publication Data
Thomason, Lezette,
   Victorian elegance / Lezette Thomason
      p.   cm.
   Includes bibliographical references and index.
   ISBN 1-56477-159-8
   1. Patchwork—Patterns. 2. Quilting—Patterns. 3. Crazy quilts. 4. Decoration and ornament—Victorian style.
   I. Title.
TT835.T48   1996
746.46'041—dc20   96-16465
                                              CIP

DEDICATION
To Anne

"Always look for the silver lining and try to find the sunny side of life."

—Sir Pelham Grenville Wodehouse (1881–1975)

ACKNOWLEDGMENTS

I would like to respectfully acknowledge:

Annette White, my ever-encouraging twin sister, who is generous with computer help and who has promised to be my roommate in the "old-age home";

Cathy Jones, my friend, who has always been there when I needed her;

Louise Armstrong, my mother, from whom I inherited my innate sense of sewing concepts and my silver hair;

Robert F. Armstrong, my father, who has shown the courage of a pride of lions;

Mary Frank King, whose creativity has inspired me to spread my own wings;

Ginger Caldwell, for her insistence on stability;

Martha Coulam, who shared her beautiful Montana home where I could quietly work on some of these needlework projects;

Margaret Taylor, who encouraged me to put these projects into a book;

Blanche McClure, who represented the essence of the gracious Southern lady during my awkward teenage years;

Melissa Lowe, for her excellent editorial guidance;

Laurel Strand, for beautiful artwork;

and finally, Michael Thomason, my writer-golfer-lawyer husband and my best friend, who has held my world together for a number of years now.

Contents

Introduction

I grew up in the rural, small-town South, where sewing, embroidery, quilting, gardening, and canning have been and still are part of everyday life. A great-grandmother taught me to crochet. A grandmother taught me to hand quilt. My mother taught me to sew.

Although I have been a city girl for twenty-five years, sewing, embroidery, quilting, and gardening are still an essential part of my life. Today, I have a flower garden instead of a vegetable garden. It's fun to bring the blossoms from my flower garden into my stitching. Crazy patchwork is the perfect place for this. Each oddly shaped piece of fabric is a little canvas just waiting to be "painted" with stitches from nature.

My friends and family complimented my designs and encouraged me to put them together in this book. I am very pleased That Patchwork Place has chosen to publish *Victorian Elegance*.

History

Crazy-patch quilts—what a hodge-podge of colors, fabrics, and textures! Victorian-style crazy quilts have been popular since the 1870s, when a lady's fine linens were a reflection of her gentility. A crazy quilt was an opportunity for a woman to display her expertise with needle and thread, as well as her position in the community, and a place where she could record special events in her life.

In well-to-do homes, women recycled rich brocade, plush velvet, precious silk, and fine linen, and used these fabrics as the foundation for intricate needlework. They might have used silk from a wedding dress, batiste from a christening gown, linen from a groom's shirt, or damask from a grandmother's cherished table linens. In less-well-to-do homes, women dressed up old clothing, fabric scraps, and flour sacks with fine stitchery.

A crazy quilt was a very personal creation. An artistic needlewoman could tell all the important events of her life. These quilts recorded births, marriages, and friendships with exquisite embroidery. The finished quilt was a source of pride for the quiltmaker and her family.

How To Use This Book

 hope this book provides you with an opportunity to enjoy the history and tradition of Victorian crazy patch and embroidery as well as to create something very personal for yourself or a loved one.

The first part of this book is a guide to choosing fabrics, threads, needles, and buttons. The many different fabrics form the canvas on which you will paint your stitches. There is an enormous array of threads, yarns, and cords you can use—anything you can thread through a needle or couch with another thread.

The second part of this book is a guide to crazy patchwork and embroidery stitches. Crazy patchwork is made of oddly shaped fabric pieces randomly sewn together. This book includes three easy crazy-patch methods. Choose the method that best suits the project you want to make, then choose from the many simple stitches, combination stitches, flower-garden stitches, and whimsies to embellish the patchwork.

The ten projects in the third part of this book offer something for everyone. The ruffled pillow, picture frames, footstool cover, and Christmas stocking are beautiful projects for home decorating. All the projects make wonderful gifts for a bride, friend, or family member. It may be hard to decide which to make first!

Tip

COUCHING

To "couch" a thread, you use small stitches of a fine thread to sew a second thread flat. For examples of couching, see "Clematis" (page 27) and "Spiderweb" (page 32).

Materials And Supplies

nlike nineteenth-century crazy patchwork, the projects in this book include only one color of fabric for the background. For example, if you chose a deep pine green as the background for a holiday purse, you would look for pine green linen, silk, velveteen, jacquard, and moiré. Each of these fabrics has a different "look" or visual texture that sets it apart from the others.

I have included sources for all kinds of fabric and thread in "Resources" on page 76. But please don't feel that you must invest in the more exotic fabrics and threads—the beauty of these projects and quilts rises from the heart and hands of the maker.

FOUNDATION MATERIAL

All of the crazy-patch methods in this book are based on a stabilizer—the foundation on which you sew the crazy-patch pieces. There are many different stabilizers and foundation materials. The weight or stiffness of the stabilizer is based on the desired weight or stiffness of the finished project. For example, you need a heavy-weight stabilizer for the scissors case. When you look at stabilizer and foundation materials, remember you must be able to pull a needle with a variety of threads through it. I have suggested a weight in each project. I recommend muslin, Sew-in Durapress (a woven interfacing from Prym Dritz), Sheer Mist shadow voile (woven interfacing), Pellon® #910 lightweight interfacing, and Pellon #930 heavy-weight interfacing.

FABRICS

One of the nice things about these projects is you need only small pieces of fabric, which means you can give that expensive silk or Ultra Suede® a second look. (An eighth of a yard doesn't cost that much!) Look for fabric at quilt, drapery, upholstery, and fabric shops. Many of these fabrics are also available from mail-order suppliers; see "Resources" on page 76. And don't forget your scrap bag. If you hem your husband's pants, save that little piece of wool flannel or twill. Someday, it will be just what you need.

Before you begin a project, think about the look you want for the finished piece. These projects can have a formal, casual, feminine, or masculine look, depending on the types of fabrics you choose. Use the following to help you choose fabric for the look you want.

Brocade is floral-patterned fabric with a raised design woven from a different fiber (or metallic yarns). The pattern is usually a different color from the background. Brocade has a rich, dressy look.

Burlap is a coarse fabric with a loose basket weave made of jute, hemp, or cotton. It's a good idea to use a stabilizer with burlap because of the very loose weave. Burlap is perfect for casual and masculine projects.

Corduroy is a durable fabric made of cotton or a cotton/polyester blend. It is available in a variety of weights and wales (the parallel ridges on one side of the fabric). The width of the wales, ranging from narrow to wide, determines the texture and look. Corduroy is wonderful for a casual project.

Cotton, the quilter's staple, has a smooth texture. A highly polished cotton can have a dressy look. Cotton muslin makes a good stabilizer.

Damask is usually made of linen. It has a woven design, similar to jacquard, that is reversible. A damask napkin is a wonderful fabric for an "old linens" project, especially as the background for a Ruffled Fans Pillow. (See photos on pages 33 and 34.)

Duck is a heavy, densely woven cotton fabric. It is good for masculine projects.

Faille can be made of silk, acetate, or a blend of those fibers. It has tiny horizontal lines or ribbing, similar to moiré but without the watermarking. Faille has a dressy look; use it for an elegant project.

Jacquard is usually made of cotton, silk, linen, or blends of those fibers. It is a heavily figured cloth with the design woven into the fabric. The woven design gives it good texture for casual or formal projects—based on the fiber content.

Linen, made from flax (pure linen), rayon, or silk, has a regular weave. The weight and texture of the cloth is based on the thread size and count. Light- and medium-weight linen has a more casual look; heavier, finely woven linen has an elegant look.

Moiré, made of either cotton, acetate, or a blend of these fibers, has a watermark pattern. It is wonderful for a more formal piece. The weight of moiré makes it a good choice for covering picture-frame backs and stands.

Piqué is a cotton or cotton/polyester blend. This fabric has a woven pattern of raised ribs or waffles. Piqué is good with tone-on-tone cottons in a casual project.

Plissé is a cotton fabric with a crinkled look; this texture is great in a casual project with tone-on-tone cottons.

Satin is available in a tremendous variety of fibers, weights, and finishes. It can have a high sheen or soft, lustrous finish. Use satin in a dressy or formal project.

Silk is available in a variety of weights and finishes. For example, silk Charmeuse has a very smooth finish; messaline has a twill finish; and douppioni, which is made from irregular silk yarn, contains slubs or irregular lumps. All silks work well in elegant projects. Heavier-weight spun silks, which are made from irregular pieces of silk yarn, are wonderful in casual or masculine pieces.

Taffeta, often made of synthetic fibers, has a smooth finish. It's changeable color gives it a dressy look.

Twill is a type of weave available in cotton, silk, and wool. Twill fabrics are tremendously durable. Use twills for casual or masculine projects.

Ultra Suede® is a synthetic fiber that resembles suede leather. It is great for masculine projects. Suede cloth is much less expensive and also works well.

Velvet is made of silk or a synthetic fiber. It has a deep pile and feels very luxurious. Velveteen or cotton velvet is a beautiful low-pile fabric. Use these for formal or casual projects, based on the weight and look of the fabric.

Viyella® is a twill-weave, cotton and wool fabric that looks like 100% wool. Viyella works well in casual pieces.

Wool, like silk, is available in a variety of weights and finishes. For example, boiled wool and camel's hair are heavier-weight with a soft look. Wool works best in a less dressy piece.

TI P

ANTIQUE LINENS

Do you have any of your grand-mother's linens? Many of us have hand-embroidered doilies and dresser scarves. You can also find old linens at antique shops and flea markets—sometimes at bargain prices. These treasures make lovely crazy-patch projects, and much of the embroidery work has already been done.

THREADS

The size of the thread, yarn, ribbon, or cord determines how heavy or delicate your embroidery will look. Needlepoint specialty shops, craft stores, needle-arts mail-order companies, and fabric stores are good sources for specialty threads. (See "Resources" on page 76.) The following lists some of your choices. I encourage you to be resourceful and inventive in your combinations. There are no rules!

Bouclé is a rayon cord from Mokuba that has high sheen and fabulous texture.

Chenille thread has a wonderful, fuzzy, casual appearance that is great for masculine projects.

Cotton embroidery floss has six strands and a matte finish. Use the strands singly or in multiples. This floss is great for stems, small leaves, and bug legs.

Linen thread, such as Rainbow Linen, has a soft sheen. Rainbow Linen, made in Sweden, is available in the United States. You can also pull a thread from a piece of linen fabric. Linen thread is great for a masculine project.

Machine embroidery thread, such as Sulky®, has a high sheen and works well for delicate work.

Patina™ is a cable cord with a high luster.

Metallic embroidery thread, such as that from Sulky and J & P Coats®, is perfect for spiderwebs and bug legs. It has a high sheen.

Metallic cords are perfect for couched snail shells. Balger Medium #16 from Kreinik is a metallic braid made in the United States. YLI makes a similar cord. Mokuba has a metallic cord that looks like little beads strung together. It adds wonderful depth to your embroidery.

Metallic ribbon is not as pliable as silk ribbon, but it is wonderful for Christmas projects. Fyre Werks™ is available in short lengths.

Metallic yarns are also wonderful for Christmas projects, adding a slightly different texture. Cresta d'Oro™, made in Italy, can be couched for snail shells. Razzle-Dazzle, made in the United States, adds sparkle. Candlelight™, a lightweight metallic yarn, is very soft and easy to work with.

Perle cotton is a twisted cotton thread with a matte finish. I recommend using size 5 or 8. Pebbly Perle™, made in France, is a wonderful cabled cotton. Bravo! is a 4-ply cord available in variegated colors. Satin cord from Mokuba is perfect for dressy projects.

Ribbon floss is a shiny, woven thread made of rayon. It is about ⅛" wide. Ribbon floss has a heavy look when used in embroidery. Although ribbon floss can be purchased on spools, shorter lengths are available as Neon Rays™ needlepoint ribbon. It is made in Germany and is available in the United States.

Silk floss has seven strands and a pretty sheen. Use the strands singly or in multiples. I like to use silk floss from YLI.

Silk ribbon is soft and pliable. It is available in 2mm, 4mm, and 7mm widths. Silk ribbon from YLI has an elegant look that cannot be achieved with any other thread. The color variations available in overdyed silk ribbon add depth to your stitches. Mokuba makes a varigated silk ribbon with several colors in one package.

Wool yarns are great for masculine projects. The yarns can usually be divided when a smaller strand is desired. I often work with a variegated wool yarn called Twedie, which is made in England. Using variegated thread adds depth to your embroidery.

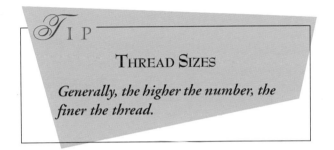

THREAD SIZES

Generally, the higher the number, the finer the thread.

BUTTONS AND BEADS

I am always looking for button "treasures" at flea markets and antique malls. For casual projects, look for buttons carved from seashells, coconut shells, and wood. For formal projects, pearl buttons in white, smoke, and other colors are perfect. Remember to look at the back of the button as well as the front; sometimes the back is more interesting and whimsical. Buttons and beads are available at most needlework and craft stores.

NEEDLES

Using the correct needle will make embroidery work easier and more enjoyable. The size of the eye, the sharpness of the point, and the diameter are important considerations.

The eye must be large enough to thread easily. If you want to pierce the fabric as you embroider, use a needle with a sharp point. If you want to go between the threads, use a needle with a blunt point. To test the diameter of the needle, thread it with silk ribbon and take a stitch in your fabric. The needle should be large enough to make a hole that silk ribbon can pass through without shredding. This is just one example; the size of the eye and diameter of the needle you need will depend on what you want to do. Another size needle might be necessary for stringing beads. Use the following as a guide to help you choose the needle for the look you want.

Beading needles (sizes 10–15) have a small eye, a sharp point, and are very long. They are great for sewing on beads. However, because beading needles bend easily, some people prefer using milliners or sharps.

Chenilles (sizes 13–26) have a sharp point and a long, enlarged eye. These needles are great for working with most types of specialty threads and yarns.

Crewels or embroidery needles (sizes 1–10) have a sharp point and a long, slender eye. These needles were designed to work with multistrand threads and yarns.

Milliners (sizes 3/0–12) have a sharp point and a small eye. They are a consistent diameter from end to end. Milliners work well with single-strand thread and for sewing on beads.

Sharps (sizes 1–12) have a sharp point and a small eye. They work well with single-strand thread and for sewing on beads.

Tapestry needles (sizes 13–26) have a blunt point and a long, enlarged eye. They do not snag or pierce the threads of the fabric. Use tapestry needles for silk ribbon or cord.

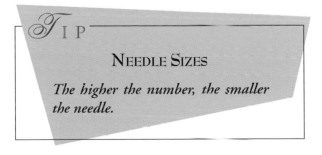

NEEDLE SIZES

The higher the number, the smaller the needle.

"She whisked about all day with rainbow-hued swatches of cloth in wool silk canvas felt denim linen chintz dangling from her fingers, stuffing her handbags, pinned crazy-quilt fashion to the front of her dress, no one was safe from her happy plan."

—Edna Ferber, *Giant*, 1952

Crazy Patchwork

This book includes three methods for creating a crazy-patch background. In the first method, you work from a corner of the foundation, adding rows of pieces. In the second method, you work from the center of the foundation, adding pieces in a spiral. In the third method, you use the pattern to make a crazy-patch background exactly like the sample project. Try each method to determine which you prefer. I have included recommendations when one method works better than another for a specific project.

WORKING FROM A CORNER

1. Cut stabilizer or muslin the size of the finished project plus seam or turn-over allowances.

2. Cut a piece of fabric that has at least five sides; this is piece #1. Place piece #1, right side up, on one corner of the foundation and pin.

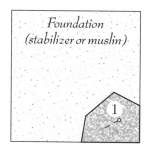

3. From a different fabric, cut piece #2. The shape is not important. With right sides together, place piece #2 on piece #1. Align one edge of the two pieces of fabric and stitch. Fold piece #2 to the right side and press. Do not worry if excess fabric hangs off the foundation; you will trim it later.

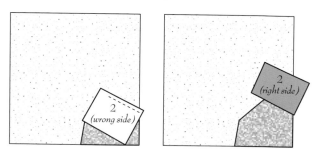

4. From a different fabric, cut piece #3. With right sides together, place piece #3 on pieces #1 and #2. Align one edge of piece #3 with an unsewn edge of piece #1 and stitch as shown in step 3. Trim the seam allowance to ¼" if necessary. Fold piece #3 to the right side and press.

5. From a different fabric, cut piece #4. With right sides together, place piece #4 on pieces #1–#3. Align one edge of piece #4 with another unsewn edge of piece #1 and stitch. Trim the seam allowance to ¼" if necessary. Fold piece #4 to the right side and press. Your first row, pieces #1–4, is complete.

6. Start the second row on the opposite side from the first row. Cut a different piece of fabric and place it, right sides together, on piece #4. Stitch.

Fold piece #5 to the right side and press. Trim the seam allowance to ¼" if necessary.

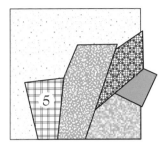

7. Continue stitching pieces of fabric to the foundation as described in steps 2–6. Try not to place pieces of the same type of fabric together. Start each new row on the opposite side from where you started the previous row.

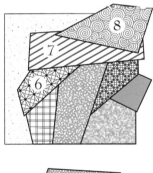

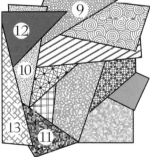

8. When you have completely covered the foundation with crazy patch, turn it over to the foundation side. Staystitch ⅛" from the edge of the foundation. Trim the fabric even with the foundation.

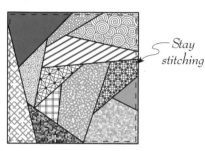

Stay stitching

WORKING FROM THE CENTER

1. Cut stabilizer or muslin the size of the finished project plus seam or turn-over allowances.

2. Cut a piece of fabric that has five sides; this is piece #1. Place piece #1, right side up, in the center of the foundation and pin.

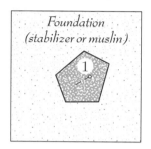

Foundation (stabilizer or muslin)

3. From a different fabric, cut piece #2. The shape is not important. With right sides together, place piece #2 on piece #1. Align one edge of the two pieces of fabric and stitch. Fold piece #2 to the right side and press.

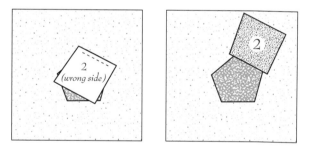

4. From a different fabric, cut piece #3. With right sides together, place piece #3 on pieces #1 and #2. Align one edge of piece #3 with an unsewn edge of piece #1 and stitch as shown in step 3, letting the stitching extend over piece #2. Trim the seam allowance to ¼" if necessary. Fold piece #3 to the right side and press.

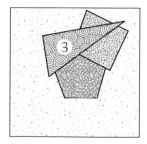

5. From a different fabric, cut piece #4. With right sides together, place piece #4 on pieces #1–#3. Align one edge of piece #4 with an unsewn edge of piece #1 and stitch. Trim the seam allowance to ¼" if necessary. Fold piece #4 to the right side and press.

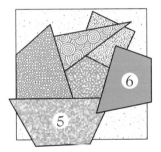

6. Repeat for pieces #5 and #6. Fold over and press piece #5 before stitching piece #6. You have now stitched a spiral of fabric around piece #1.

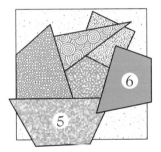

7. For the second fabric spiral, work in the opposite direction. From a different piece of fabric, cut piece #7 and place it, right sides together, on pieces #5 and #6. Stitch. Trim the seam allowance to ¼" if necessary. Fold piece #7 to the right side and press.

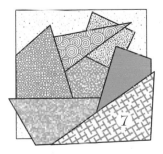

8. Continue stitching fabric pieces to the foundation as described in steps 2–7. Try not to place pieces of the same type of fabric together. For each new fabric spiral, work in the opposite direction from the previous spiral.

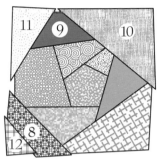

9. When you have completely covered the foundation with crazy patch spirals, turn it over to the foundation side. Staystitch ⅛" from the edge of the foundation. Trim the fabric even with the foundation.

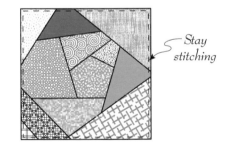

Stay stitching

PATTERN PIECING

You can use this method to make a crazy-patch background exactly like the project instead of sewing together randomly cut pieces. To pattern piece, trace the guide on tissue paper, reverse it, and trace it on a foundation before stitching the fabric pieces to the back side of the foundation. *It's important to reverse the guide before stitching (see step 2 below).* This step is particularly important for the Christmas stocking.

Use the pattern guide below to piece a small background. It is the correct size for a Christmas ornament as shown on pages 40 and 41.

1. Trace the guide on tissue paper.

2. Turn over the tissue paper and trace the guide on the back side.

3. Place the stabilizer or muslin on the back side of the tissue paper and trace the guide onto the foundation. (If necessary, use a light table or window to help trace the guide.) Stitch the fabric to the foundation, not the tissue paper.

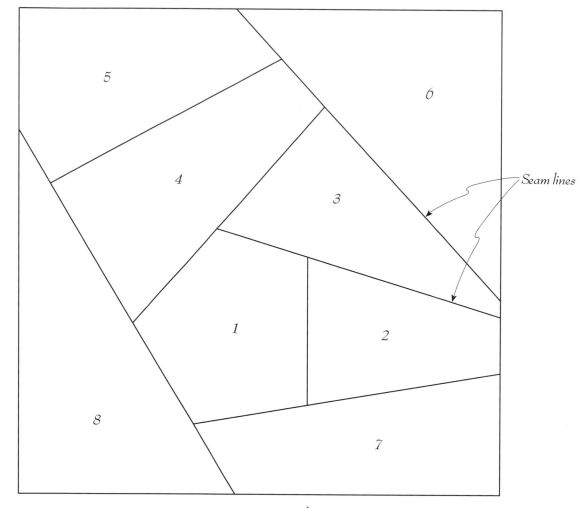

Pattern Piecing Guide
Trace and reverse before stitching.

4. Cut a piece of fabric at least ¼" larger around than piece #1 on the guide. Place this piece, right side up, so it covers piece #1 on the foundation and pin. Make sure the fabric extends beyond the pattern lines at least ¼".

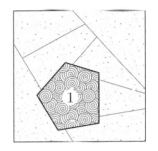

Place piece #1 on the foundation (stabilizer or muslin).

5. From a different fabric, cut a piece at least ¼" larger around than piece #2 on the guide. Place this piece, right sides together, on piece #1. Stitch on the seam line. Trim the seam allowance to ¼" if necessary. Fold piece #2 to the right side and press.

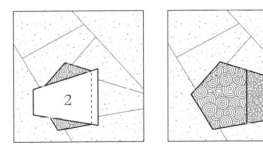

Place piece #2 on piece #1, right sides together, and stitch.

6. From a different fabric, cut a piece at least ¼" larger around than piece #3 on the guide. Place this piece, right sides together, on pieces #1 and #2. With the foundation right side up, stitch on

the seam line as shown in step 5. Trim the seam allowance to ¼" if necessary. Fold piece #3 to the right side and press.

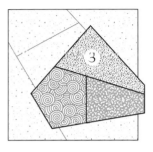

7. From a different fabric, cut a piece at least ¼" larger around than piece #4 on the guide. Place this piece, right sides together, on pieces #1 and #3. With the foundation right side up, stitch on the seam line. Trim the seam allowance to ¼" if necessary. Fold piece #4 to the right side and press.

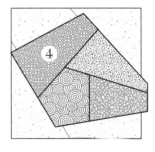

8. From a different fabric, cut a piece at least ¼" larger around than piece #5 on the guide. Place this piece, right sides together, on piece #4. With the foundation right side up, stitch on the seam line. Trim the seam allowance to ¼" if necessary Fold piece #5 to the right side and press.

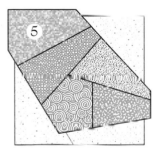

9. From a different fabric, cut a piece at least ¼" larger around than piece #6 on the guide. Place this piece, right sides together, on pieces #3, #4, and #5. With the foundation right side up, stitch on the seam line. Trim the seam allowance to ¼" if necessary. Fold piece #6 to the right side and press.

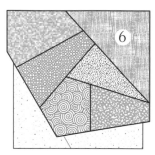

10. From a different fabric, cut a piece at least ¼" larger around than piece #7 on the guide. Place this piece, right sides together, on pieces #1 and #2. With the foundation right side up, stitch on the seam line. Trim the seam allowance to ¼" if necessary. Fold piece #7 to the right side and press.

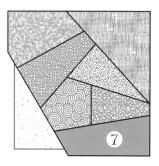

11. From a different fabric, cut a piece at least ¼" larger around than piece #8 on the guide. Place this piece, right sides together, on pieces #4, #1, and #7. With the foundation right side up, stitch on the seam line. Trim the scam allowance to ¼" if necessary. Fold piece #8 to the right side and press.

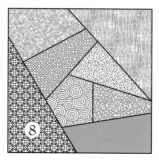

12. When you have completely covered the foundation with crazy patchwork, turn it over to the foundation side. Staystitch ⅛" from the edge of the foundation. Turn it back over to the crazy-patch side and trim the fabric even with the foundation.

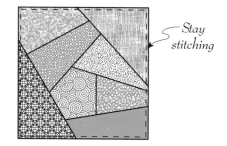

Stay stitching

Embroidery

The stitches included here represent only a few of those created for embroidery. I encourage you to use your imagination to create more. The books listed in "Suggested Reading" on page 75 are excellent sources for additional embroidery stitches.

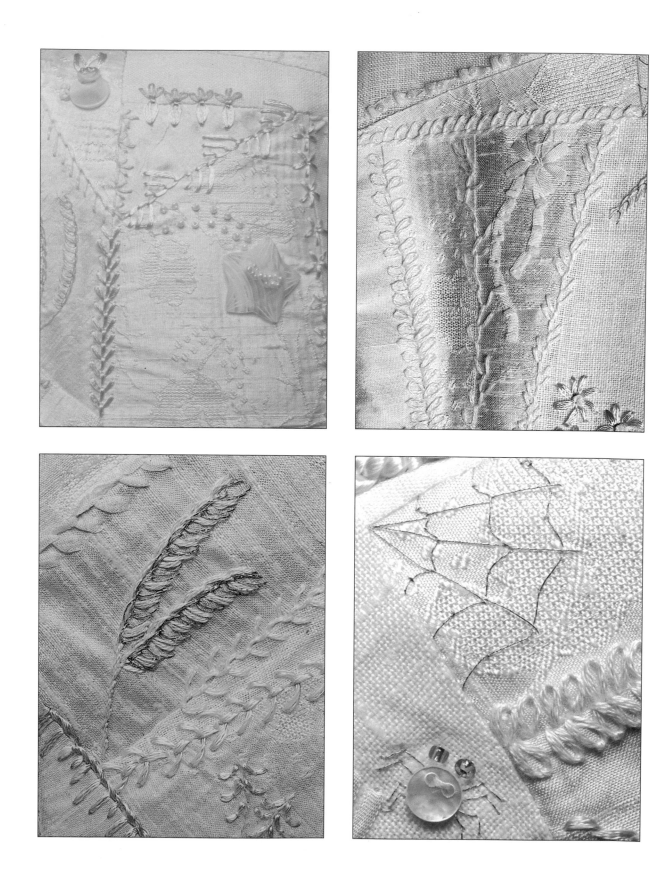

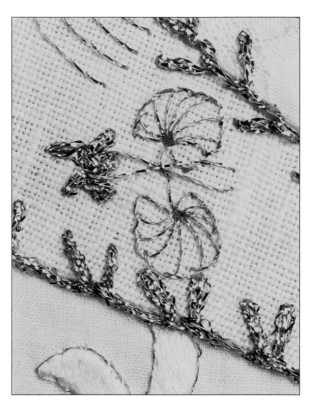

19

SIMPLE STITCHES

Backstitch

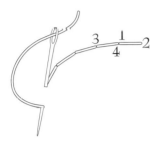

Bullion Stitch

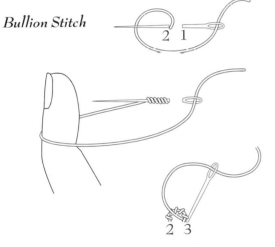

Finished bullion

Buttonhole Stitch

BUTTONHOLE STITCH VARIATIONS

Buttonhole Stitch, Alternating

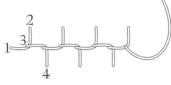

Buttonhole Stitch with Short-Long-Short Stitches, Alternating

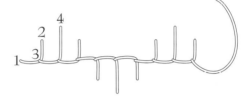

Buttonhole Stitch with Short-Long-Short Stitches and Ribbon Stitch, Alternating

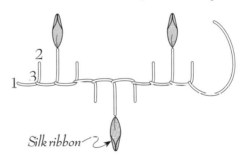

Silk ribbon

Buttonhole Stitch with Short-Medium-Long-Medium-Short Stitches

*Buttonhole Stitch with Short-Medium-Long-
Medium-Short Stitches, Alternating*

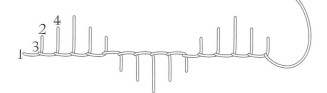

Buttonhole Stitch with Two Stitch Lengths

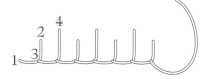

Double Slanted Buttonhole Stitch, Alternating

Single Detached Buttonhole Stitch, Alternating

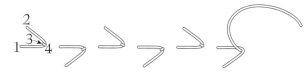

Slanted Buttonhole Stitch

Slanted Buttonhole Stitch, Alternating

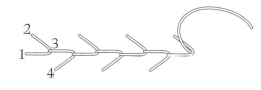

Triple Slanted Buttonhole Stitch, Alternating

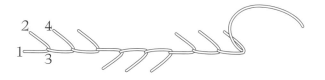

Crow's Foot Stitch

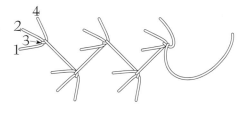

Fern Stitch

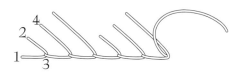

Fern Stitch, Alternating

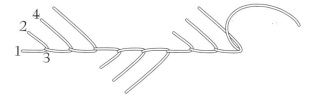

22

French Knot

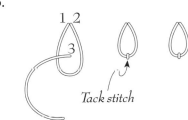

Finished French knot

Fly Stitch

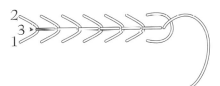

Grass Stitch (Three Straight Stitches from One Point)

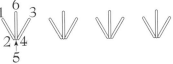

Grass Stitch (Five Straight Stitches from One Point)

Lazy Daisy Stitch

Use a tack stitch to hold down the end of the loop.

Tack stitch

Ribbon Stitch

At the end of each stitch, make a loop and pull the ribbon to curl the edges around the point. If you pull the ribbon too tightly, the curls will disappear.

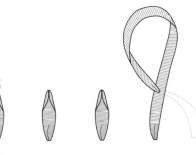

Ribbon Stitch, Looped

At the end of each stitch, make a loose loop. This looks like a curled petal.

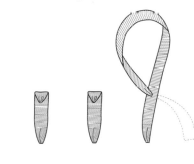

Rickrack Stitch

Work this stitch like a **X** stitch, making the first line of stitches, then making the second line of stitches.

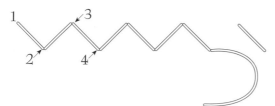

Running Ribbon Stitch

At the end of each stitch, make a loop and pull the ribbon to curl the edges around the point. If you pull the ribbon too tightly, the curls will disappear.

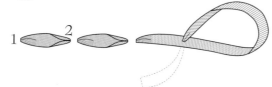

Running Ribbon Stitch, Looped

At the end of each stitch, make a loose loop.

Running Stitch with Ribbon

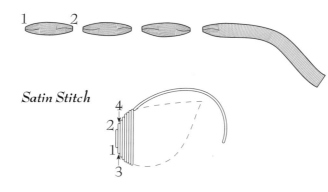

Satin Stitch

Tree Stitch

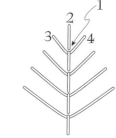

Tree Stitch with Ribbon

Triple Lazy Daisy Stitch

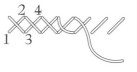

X Stitch

Zigzagged Fly Stitch

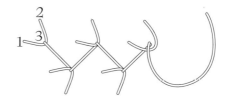

COMBINATION STITCHES

Buttonhole Stitch with Beads or French Knots, Alternating

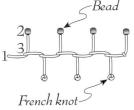

Buttonhole Stitch with Short-Medium-Long-Medium-Short Stitches with Beads or French Knots, Alternating

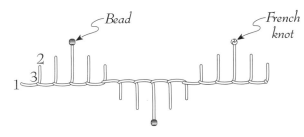

Fern Stitch with Beads or French Knots, Alternating

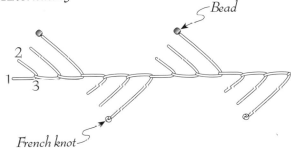

Fern Stitch with Grass Stitch (Three Stitches)

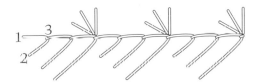

Fern Stitch with Single Slanted Buttonhole Stitch

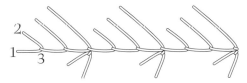

Grass Stitch (Three Stitches) with Beads or French Knots

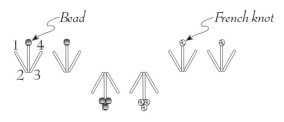

Grass Stitch (Five Stitches) with Beads or French Knots

Looped Ribbon Stitch with Beads or French Knots

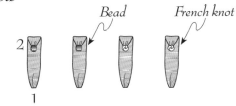

Rickrack Stitch with Beads or French Knots

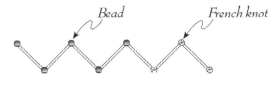

25

Rickrack Stitch with Bugle Beads

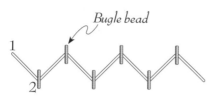

Bugle bead

1

2

Running Stitch with Ribbon, Beads, French Knots, and Lazy Daisy Stitches

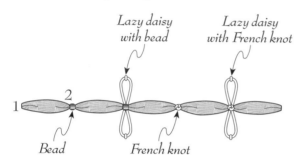

Lazy daisy with bead

Lazy daisy with French knot

2

1

Bead

French knot

Single Slanted Buttonhole Stitch with Beads or French Knots

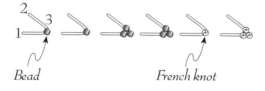

2   3

1

Bead

French knot

Slanted Buttonhole Stitch with Beads or French Knots, Alternating

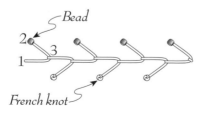

Bead

2

3

1

French knot

Slanted Buttonhole Stitch with Lazy Daisy Stitches and Beads or French Knots, Alternating

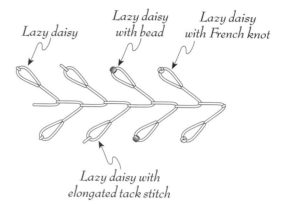

Lazy daisy

Lazy daisy with bead

Lazy daisy with French knot

Lazy daisy with elongated tack stitch

Straight Stitch with Lazy Daisy Leaves and Beads, French Knots, or Buttonhole Flowers

Bead

French knots

2

1

Buttonhole

Buttonhole with bead

Buttonhole with French knot

Triple Lazy Daisy Stitch with Beads or French Knots

Bead

French knots

"Won't you come into my garden?
I would like my roses to see you."
—Richard Brinsley Sheridan (1751–1816),
To a Young Lady

FLOWER–GARDEN STITCHES

These artistic flowers represent only a small number of the many you can stitch. Remember that you can give a flower different looks by using different types of thread!

Black-Eyed Susan

Use ribbon stitches with silk ribbon to make the petals. Use a bead or French knot to make the flower center.

—Bead

Branch with Leaves

Use an alternating fly stitch to make the branch. Use straight stitches with silk ribbon to make the leaves.

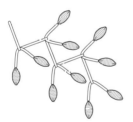

Cattail

Use a bullion stitch to make the cattail spikes. Use long straight stitches to make the stem and leaves.

Christmas Tree

Backstitch the tree outline, then decorate the tree with French knots or bead balls.

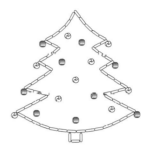

Clematis

To make the stem, couch a straight stitch. Use lazy daisy stitches to make the leaves, and lazy daisy stitches with an elongated tack stitch to make the petals. Use a cluster of beads or French knots to make the flower center.

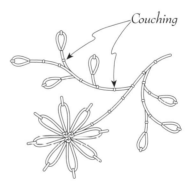

Couching

Crocus

To make the stem and leaves, couch straight stitches. To make the petals, use straight stitches with silk ribbon, then couch the silk ribbon with one strand of embroidery floss.

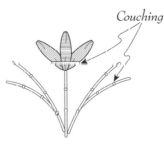

Couching

Daffodil

To make the stem and leaves, couch straight stitches. Use 2mm silk ribbon, ribbon floss, or embroidery floss to make the petals. Use two looped ribbon stitches with silk ribbon to make the flower cup.

Couching

Daisy

To make the stem, couch a straight stitch. Use straight stitches or ribbon stitches with silk ribbon to make the petals. Use a cluster of beads or French knots to make the flower center.

Couching

Daisy with Ribbon Streamers

To make the petals and ribbon streamers, use ribbon stitches with silk ribbon. Use a bead or French knot to make the flower center.

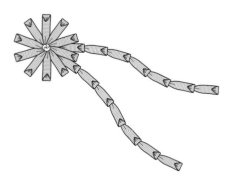

Dandelion

To make the stem, couch a straight stitch. Use elongated lazy daisy stitches to make the leaves and flowers.

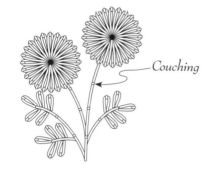

Couching

Fern

To make the stem, couch straight stitches. Use elongated lazy daisy stitches for the fronds. For best results, use a fine thread to embroider ferns.

Foxglove

Use a backstitch to make the stem, and lazy daisy stitches for the leaves. For best results, use one strand of thread. To make the flowers, use looped ribbon stitches with silk ribbon.

Goldenrod

Use a backstitch to make the stem, and lazy daisy stitches for the leaves. For best results, use one strand of thread. To make the flowers, use straight stitches with silk ribbon or ribbon floss.

Grape Hyacinth

Use a cluster of beads or French knots for the flowers, and straight stitches for the leaves.

Iris

Use straight stitches to make the stem and leaves. For the top petals, use lazy daisy stitches. For the bottom petals, use straight stitches and ribbon stitches with silk ribbon.

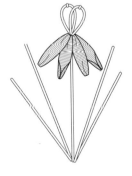

Pussy Willow

To make the branch, use a randomly alternating buttonhole stitch. For best results, use one strand of thread. Use beads or French knots to make the buds.

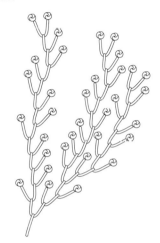

Snowdrop

Use straight stitches to make the stem, leaves, and petals. Use silk ribbon, ribbon floss, or metallic ribbon for the petals.

Tree, Ribbon

With silk ribbon or ribbon floss, use a fly stitch to make the tree. Increase the length of each stitch as shown.

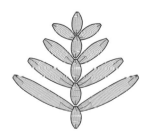

29

Trees in a Row

To make a row of trees, use a fly stitch and increase the length of each stitch as shown. For best results, use one strand of thread.

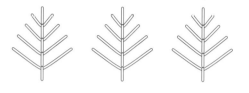

Tulips

To make the stem, couch straight stitches. Use elongated lazy daisy stitches to make the leaves. For best results, use one strand of thread. Use a looped ribbon stitch with silk ribbon to make the petals.

Violets

To make the stem, couch straight stitches. Use a buttonhole stitch from one point to make the leaves, and straight stitches to make the petals.

Wheat

Using one strand of thread and a slanted buttonhole stitch, work one line of stitches on a curve as shown. Using a different colored thread, work a second line of buttonhole stitches over the first. Repeat for the third line.

Windflowers

To make the petals, use straight stitches with silk ribbon, ribbon floss, or metallic ribbon. Use a cluster of beads or French knots to make the flower center.

Wisteria or Grape Cluster

To make the vine, use straight and elongated lazy daisy stitches as shown. Use beads or French knots to make the blossoms or grapes.

WHIMSIES

Whimsies are wonderful little creatures that add a quaint or fanciful touch to a piece of needlework. Generally made with flat pearl buttons or satin-stitch bodies, use your imagination—along with your button and fiber collection—to create a menagerie.

Beetle

Use a satin stitch or button for the body, beads for the eyes, and a straight stitch for the legs and antennae. Make two French knots at the ends of the antennae. Metallic thread is great for the legs and antennae.

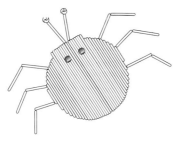

Bird in a Nest

To make the nest, use straight stitches as shown. You can use a satin stitch or button to make the bird. Use a bead or French knot for the eye.

Bunny and Carrots

To make the bunny, you need a large button with off-center eyes for the body and a small button with off-center eyes for the head. Overlap these slightly as shown. Use beads to make the eyes and a cluster of beads or French knots to make the tail. To make the ears and carrots, use an elongated lazy daisy stitch. Use a grass stitch (three straight stitches) to make the carrot tops.

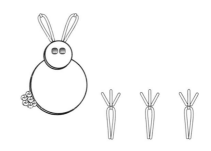

Fish

I like to use white- or smoke-colored fish-shaped buttons. Use a single fish in a small area or a school of fish in a larger area. You can also use a satin stitch to make fish. Use a bead or French knot for the eye.

Fish, Round Button

Begin this fish by sewing on a round button with contrasting-color thread. This will be the fin. (Look at the wrong side of the button; it may make a more interesting fish.) Bring 6 strands of embroidery floss up through the fabric where you want the tail to begin. Wrap the embroidery floss around the edge of the button, couching it with one strand of floss. Use straight or fly stitches to make the tail. Use a bead or French knot for the eye.

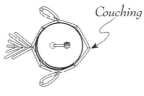

Couching

Flying Birds

Use silk ribbon and straight stitches to make flying birds. Use a bead or French knot for the head.

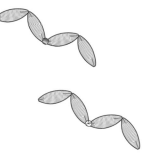

Leaf

To make the leaf, use a leaf-shaped button or satin stitch. Use silk ribbon and a straight stitch to make the stem. End with a ribbon stitch.

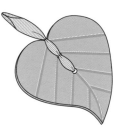

Peach

To make a peach, stitch pearls or beads on top of a button with off-center eyes (or use a satin stitch) while stitching the button to the fabric. Use silk ribbon to make the leaves, working with straight and lazy daisy stitches.

Shooting Star

To make a shooting star, stitch pearls or beads on top of a large, star-shaped button (or use a satin stitch) while stitching the button to the fabric. Stitch a double line of pearls or beads trailing from one side.

Snail

To make the snail shell, couch the cording in a close spiral as shown. Use a bead for the head. To make the body and antennae, use straight stitches. Make two French knots at the ends of the antennae.

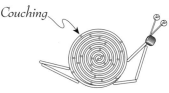

Couching

Spiderweb with Spider

To make the web, couch a strand of thread as shown. Use a satin stitch or button for the body, beads for the eyes, and a straight stitch for the legs. Metallic thread is great for the web and legs.

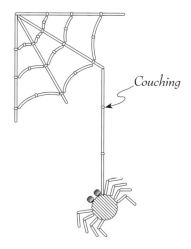

Couching

Gallery

Indigo Ruffled Fans Pillow and Footstool

LEZETTE THOMASON
NASHVILLE, TENNESSEE, 1995

What a wonderful way to show off your needlework skills! This pillow and footstool make great accessories for any home. If you choose a neutral color, these projects blend into the color scheme of the room. If you choose an accent color, these projects stand alone as a work of art. For a detail of the footstool, see page 44.

Trousseau Ruffled Fans Pillow and Lingerie Bag

LEZETTE THOMASON
NASHVILLE, TENNESSEE, 1994

These silk, lace, and linen accessories add a luxurious touch to a lady's boudoir. The lingerie bag would make an exquisite gift for a bride.

Trousseau Evening Bag and Book Cover

LEZETTE THOMASON
NASHVILLE, TENNESSEE, 1994

This lovely evening bag is perfect for the mother of the bride, a night on the town, or any special occasion. Make a crazy-patch book cover as a pretty keepsake for a mother or aunt, or for a bride's prayer book.

Trousseau Eyeglasses and Scissors Cases

LEZETTE THOMASON
NASHVILLE, TENNESSEE, 1994

An eyeglasses case is a necessity for anyone who wears glasses, so this quick project is perfect for you or as a gift for a special friend. A scissors case is a marvelous way to protect your scissors and, like the eyeglasses case, makes a quick gift.

Antique Linens Pillow, Lingerie Bag, and Frame

LEZETTE THOMASON, NASHVILLE, TENNESSEE, 1995

Made from antique linens stitched by loving hands, this pillow, lingerie bag, and frame are certain to be treasured.

Blushing Pink
Lingerie Bag

LEZETTE THOMASON
NASHVILLE, TENNESSEE, 1995

Like the Trousseau Lingerie
Bag (page 34), this lovely pink
lingerie bag is a wonderful
way to indulge yourself
or a special bride.

Autumn Picture Frames

LEZETTE THOMASON, NASHVILLE, TENNESSEE, 1995

A crazy-patch picture frame can have a formal or casual look.
These frames feature camel- and fawn-colored fabrics, and are
embroidered in soft autumn colors. The spider, beetle, and fish
buttons are attached wrong side up to show off unusual and
interesting patterns. For another detail, see page 39.

Autumn Book Cover

LEZETTE THOMASON, NASHVILLE, TENNESSEE, 1995

A crazy-patch book cover makes this an elegant
accessory in any room   instead of a book that did not
get put away. This project is a great way to use your
needlework skills to make a special gift
for the men in your family.

Festive Holiday Ornaments

LEZETTE THOMASON
NASHVILLE, TENNESSEE, 1995

These Christmas ornaments will be keepsakes to enjoy and admire for many holiday seasons. Easy to make, this project is perfect to hang on your tree or to embellish a holiday package. For a detail, see page 41.

Formal Christmas Stocking

LEZETTE THOMASON
NASHVILLE, TENNESSEE, 1995

What a treasure to hang by the fireplace each holiday season! This Christmas stocking is crazy patched in pine green and lamé fabrics and embellished with metallic gold thread for holiday flare. Gold charms add a whimsical touch.

Emerald and Sable Evening Bags

LEZETTE THOMASON, NASHVILLE, TENNESSEE, 1995

Shimmering with embroidery, beads, and whimsies, these evening bags bespeak a more graceful era.
Fancy cording finishes the edges and extends into a shoulder strap. A tassel attached on one side
adds an asymmetrical touch of elegance.

Ebony Eyeglasses Case

LEZETTE THOMASON, NASHVILLE, TENNESSEE, 1995

This eyeglasses case has a crazy-patch front and can be backed with velveteen, moiré, or brocade. The case is lined with a soft fabric to avoid scratching the glasses. This is an elegant way to carry your eyeglasses to the office or the opera.

Indigo Footstool

LEZETTE THOMASON, NASHVILLE, TENNESSEE, 1995

Unlike the other projects in this book, this fun project includes more than one color of fabric. I chose indigo for the primary color, then incorporated plaids and checks with other colors I wanted. Why stop with a footstool? Consider making cushion covers for your dining room chairs. Your decor and needle skills are sure to be the envy of your friends.

Projects

All the projects in this book are easy, but some are quicker to finish than others. The projects with large areas of crazy patchwork and embroidery, such as the lingerie bag and footstool cover, will take a little more time than the scissors case and Christmas ornament. Once you have completed the crazy patchwork and embroidery, you will stitch or use a glue gun to assemble the project. The footstool cover is ready to attach when the embroidery is complete.

> ## TIP
>
> *In the following projects, you can substitute fabric scraps for the ⅛ yd. of fabric in the "Materials" lists.*

Ruffled Fans Pillow

Finished size: 13" x 13" (not including 3"-wide ruffle)
Color photos on pages 33 and 34

MATERIALS

44"-WIDE FABRIC

½ yd. stabilizer (lightweight interfacing) or
muslin for crazy-patch foundation

⅛ yd. each of 5 to 6 different fabrics for crazy patchwork

½ yd. fabric for front and back of pillow

½ yd. muslin for backing

½ yd. fabric for ruffle*

3 yds. of 3"-wide lace for double ruffle (optional)

14" x 14" piece of low-loft batting, such as Hobbs Thermore®

Assorted embroidery floss, perle cotton, and specialty cording

Silk ribbon, 2mm and 4mm, and ribbon floss

Quilting thread

Metallic and invisible nylon thread (optional)

Assorted beads and buttons

Quilting, chenille, embroidery, tapestry, and beading needles

14" x 14" pillow form

*The pillows in this book are finished with a 3"-wide ruffle, but
you can finish a pillow with cord or piping for a different look.

All measurements include ¼"-wide seam allowances.

CRAZY PATCHWORK

Before you begin, read "Crazy Patchwork" on pages 10–16. I recommend "Pattern Piecing" for this project. Refer to the "Piecing, Embroidery, and Quilting Guide" on the pullout pattern.

1. Using the pullout pattern, trace the fans on the foundation. Add a ¼"-wide seam allowance around each fan. Cut out the fan shapes.

2. Cut and stitch wedge-shaped pieces of the assorted fabrics to the foundation.

3. Turn under the raw edges of each fan ¼" and baste.

4. From the fabric for the pillow front, cut a 14" x 14" square.

5. Arrange the fans on the pillow front, referring to the pullout pattern, and baste. Appliqué the fans to the pillow front. For appliqué instructions, I recommend the book listed on page 75.

EMBROIDERY

1. Embroider around each fan and on the crazy-patchwork seams. Refer to "Embroidery" on pages 17–32 and the pullout pattern for suggestions.

2. Embroider the pillow between the fans if desired. Do not embroider into the seam allowances around the pillow front. This adds bulk and can make it difficult to construct the pillow.

3. If desired, fill in the embroidery with beads. Use invisible nylon thread or embroidery floss in a similar color.

QUILTING

For helpful quilting instructions and tips, I recommend the books listed on page 75.

1. Mark the quilting design on the pillow front. Refer to the quilting suggestion on the pullout pattern. Do not mark or quilt the fans.

2. Layer the pillow front with batting and backing; baste.

3. Quilt the pillow front.

4. Place a terry-cloth towel on your pressing surface. Place the pillow front, right side down, on the towel and press.

CONSTRUCTION

1. From the ruffle fabric, cut three 6"-wide strips. Make bias seams as shown, then stitch the strips together. Fold the ruffle strip in half, wrong sides together, and press.

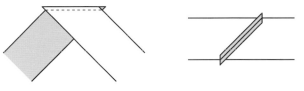

Joining Bias-Cut Strips

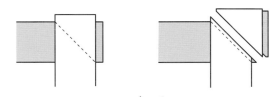

Joining Straight-Cut Strips

2. To create the ruffle, machine baste ⅜" from the raw edge of the folded strip. Leave long thread tails at the beginning and end of your stitching. Machine baste again ⅛" from the raw edge.

Gently pull the bobbin threads, working until the length of the ruffle is about the same as the perimeter of the pillow front.

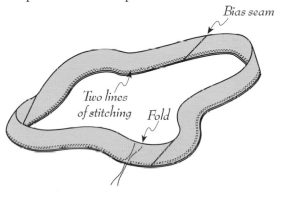

Bias seam

Two lines of stitching   *Fold*

3. Align the raw edges of the ruffle with the right side of the pillow front. Pin or baste, allowing a little extra fullness at each corner. (This keeps the corners from "cupping" or flipping up.) Stitch the ruffle to the pillow front.

Stitch ruffle to pillow front.

4. Place the pillow back and the pillow front right sides together, with the ruffle sandwiched in between. Stitch as shown, leaving a 12"-wide opening on one side.

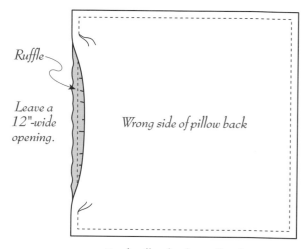

Stitch pillow back to pillow front.

5. Turn the pillow cover right side out and press if necessary.

6. Place the pillow form inside the cover. Carefully push the form into the corners. Hand stitch the opening closed.

Picture Frames

Finished sizes: 5¼" x 6¾" (3" x 5" photo), 6½" x 8½" (4" x 6" photo), and 7½" x 9¾" (5" x 7" photo)
Color photos on pages 36 and 38–39

MATERIALS

44"-WIDE FABRIC

¼ yd. stabilizer (lightweight interfacing) or muslin for crazy-patch foundation

⅛ yd. each of 5 to 6 different fabrics for crazy patchwork

⅓ yd. fabric for backing and stand

⅓ yd. Pellon® fleece

¼"-diameter decorative cording for finishing:
¾ yd. for 5¼" x 6¾" frame; 1 yd. for 6½" x 8½" frame;
1¼ yds. for 7½" x 9¾" frame

Assorted embroidery floss, perle cotton, and specialty cording

Silk ribbon, 2mm and 4mm, and ribbon floss

Metallic and invisible nylon thread (optional)

Assorted beads and buttons

Chenille, embroidery, tapestry, and beading needles

Paper or template plastic

Medium-weight art board

Ruler

Mat knife or utility knife

Glue gun or spray adhesive*

Clear tape

Sheet of clear plastic to cover photo

*Do not use fabric glue. This will soak into the fabrics, making them stiff. It may also leave circles.

All measurements include ¼"-wide seam allowances.

CRAZY PATCHWORK

Before you begin, read "Crazy Patchwork" on pages 10–16 and choose a method. I recommend "Working from a Corner" or "Pattern Piecing" for this project. Refer to the "Piecing and Embroidery Guides" on page 80 and the pullout pattern.

1. From the stabilizer or muslin, cut a rectangle 1" larger all around than the frame size. For example, cut a 9½" x 11¾" rectangle for the 7½" x 9¾" frame.

2. Cut and stitch pieces of the assorted fabrics to the foundation. You do not need to completely cover the foundation with fabric because there is no middle to the frame. Focus on creating a border.

Before stitching the last two pieces, press well. Turn under the raw edge of the last piece sewn and fold it over the first piece. Appliqué the last piece to the first piece. For appliqué instructions, I recommend the book on page 75.

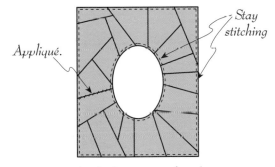

Stay stitching

Appliqué.

Finished Crazy Patchwork

EMBROIDERY

Do not embroider into the turn-under allowances around the picture frame. This adds bulk and can make it difficult to construct the frame.

1. Embroider the crazy-patchwork seams. Refer to "Embroidery" on pages 17–32 and the guide on page 80 and the pullout pattern for suggestions. If you plan to embroider a cluster or spray of flowers across a seam, you do not need to embroider the seam under the flowers.

2. If desired, fill in the embroidery with beads. Use invisible nylon thread or embroidery floss in a similar color.

3. Place a terry-cloth towel on your pressing surface. Place the crazy patchwork, right side down, on the towel and press.

CONSTRUCTION

1. Referring to page 79 and the pullout pattern, make templates for the picture frame front, back, and stand by tracing the pattern on paper or template plastic.

2. Using the templates, trace the frame front, back, and stand on medium-weight art board. Using a ruler and a mat knife, cut out the pieces of the frame. Set aside the back and stand.

3. From the Pellon fleece, cut a rectangle 1" larger all around than the frame size.

4. Using a glue gun or spray adhesive, attach the fleece to the frame front. Wrap the fleece around to the back side and glue. Trim excess fleece at corners.

5. Place the crazy patchwork, right side up, on the fleece. Wrap the crazy patchwork around to the back side of the frame front and glue. Clip the turn-over allowance where necessary.

Wrap crazy patchwork to back of art board.

Clip.

Pellon fleece

6. Using the mat knife, score the art board for the back side of the stand. Cut only halfway through the art board. Turn the board over and gently crease at the scoring line.

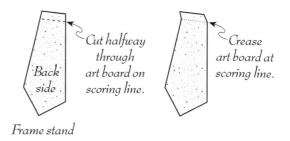

Back side

Cut halfway through art board on scoring line.

Crease art board at scoring line.

Frame stand

7. Using the templates prepared in step 1, cut fabric to cover the frame back and stand. You will need 2 pieces of fabric to cover the stand.

8. Glue the fabric to the frame back and stand. Make sure to glue the fabric to the art board at the point where the frame stand will be attached. (Otherwise, the weight of the stand will pull the fabric away from the back.) Clip the turn-over allowance where necessary.

Wrap fabric around art board.

9. Glue the frame back at the sides and bottom as shown. If you want to finish the edges of the frame with cording, leave a ½"-wide opening at the bottom.

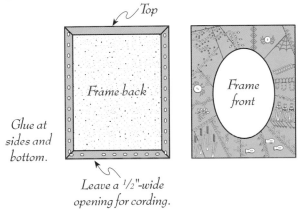

Top

Frame back

Frame front

Glue at sides and bottom.

Leave a ½"-wide opening for cording.

10. Glue the fabric to the right side of the frame stand. Clip the turn-over allowance where necessary. Trim the fabric for the back of the stand as necessary and glue as shown.

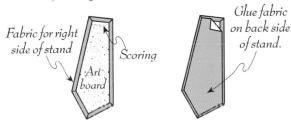

Fabric for right side of stand

Scoring

Art board

Glue fabric on back side of stand.

11. Glue the frame stand to the back side of the frame as shown.

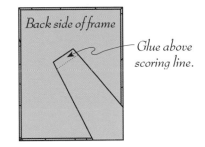

Back side of frame

Glue above scoring line.

12. Use a glue gun to attach decorative cording to the frame edges. To avoid covering the opening at the top of the frame, glue the cording to the frame front only. Use glue sparingly so the finished frame does not look messy. Wrap clear tape around the ends of the cording and trim ⅛" from the edge of the tape. Push the cording into the ½"-wide opening at the bottom of the frame and glue in place.

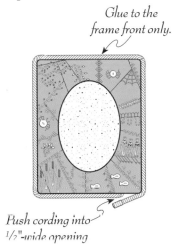

Glue to the frame front only.

Push cording into ½"-wide opening

13. Trim and insert a piece of clear plastic and a photo.

Lingerie Bag

Finished size: 13" x 14½"
Color photos on pages 34 and 36–37

Color photos on pages 34 and 36–37

"What dreadful hot weather we have! It keeps me in a continual state of inelegance."

—Jane Austen, in a letter written to her sister Cassandra in 1796

MATERIALS

44"-WIDE FABRIC

¼ yd. stabilizer (lightweight interfacing) or muslin for crazy-patch foundation

⅛ yd. each of 5 to 6 different fabrics for crazy-patch flap*

½ yd. fabric for lingerie bag

½ yd. fabric for lining

15" x 34" piece of high-loft batting (bonded)

1 ¾ yds. of ⅜"-diameter decorative cording with a ¼"-wide seam-allowance tape for finishing

1 yd. of 1"-wide satin or silk ribbon for bow

Assorted embroidery floss, perle cotton, and specialty cording

Silk ribbon, 2mm and 4mm, and ribbon floss

Metallic and invisible nylon thread (optional)

Assorted beads and buttons

Chenille, embroidery, tapestry, and beading needles

*The finished dimensions of the flap are 7" x 14½".

All measurements include ¼"-wide seam allowances.

CRAZY PATCHWORK

Before you begin, read "Crazy Patchwork" on pages 10–16 and choose a method. I recommend "Working from the Center" or "Pattern Piecing" for this project. Refer to the "Piecing and Embroidery Guide" on the pullout pattern.

1. From the stabilizer or muslin, cut a 7½" x 15" rectangle for the foundation of the crazy-patch flap.

2. Cut and stitch pieces of the assorted fabrics to the foundation. Completely cover the foundation.

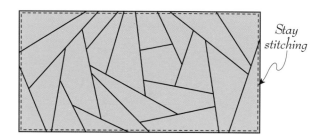

Stay stitching

Finished Crazy Patchwork

EMBROIDERY

Do not embroider into the seam allowance around the flap; this adds bulk and can make it difficult to construct the lingerie bag.

1. Embroider the crazy-patchwork seams. Refer to "Embroidery" on pages 17–32 and the pullout pattern for suggestions.

2. If desired, fill in the embroidery with beads. Use invisible nylon thread or embroidery floss in a similar color.

3. Place a terry-cloth towel on your pressing surface. Place the crazy patchwork, right side down, on the towel and press.

CONSTRUCTION

1. From the lingerie bag fabric, cut a 15" x 26½" rectangle. On the right side of the fabric, mark the center on each long side.

2. Align one long side of the flap (the top) with a short side of the 15" x 26½" rectangle as shown. With right sides together, stitch. Press the seam allowance toward the flap.

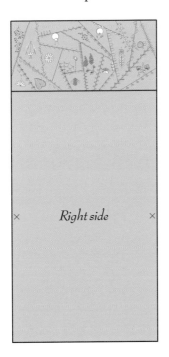

Right side

3. Align the decorative cording seam-allowance tape with the center marks on the right side of the bag fabric. Hand baste the seam-allowance tape from the center mark, up and around the flap, ending at the center mark on the other side. Clip the seam-allowance tape at the corners. Using a zipper or cording foot, machine stitch as close as possible to the cording.

Clip seam-allowance
tape at corners.

Fold line

4. Fold the bag fabric in half (at center marks), right sides together. Sew up the sides of the rectangle to the flap, ending ¼" from the edge of the bag fabric. Turn this ¼"-wide seam allowance to the wrong side and baste.

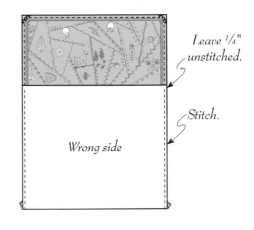

Leave ¼"
unstitched.

Stitch.

Wrong side

5. From the lining fabric, cut a 15" x 33½" rectangle. Measure and mark 13¼" on each long side.

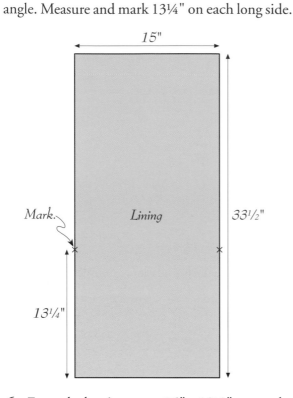

6. From the batting, cut a 15" x 13½" rectangle. Place the batting on the wrong side of the lining and tack at each corner in the seam allowance.

7. Fold the lining and batting at the marks, right sides together. Sew the sides together, ending ¼" from the raw edge.

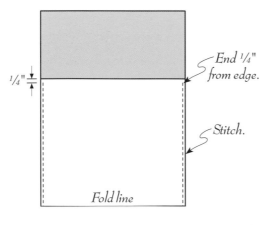

8. Align the top of the lining with the crazy-patch flap, right sides together. Pin or baste.

9. Stitch the lining to the flap, stitching on top of the seam-allowance tape. Be sure to backstitch. Carefully trim excess batting in the seam allowance to minimize bulk. Turn the lining to the right side and press gently.

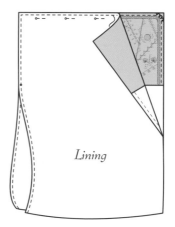

Stitch crazy-patch flap to lining.

10. Place the lining inside the bag, wrong sides together. Turn under the raw edge of the bag ¼", then hand stitch the lining to the bag.

11. Cut 2 pieces of 1"-wide ribbon, each 18" long. Measure and mark the center of the bag and the underside of the flap. Pin 1 piece of ribbon under the flap and stitch, turning under the raw edge of the ribbon. Pin the second piece on the front of the bag and stitch, again turning under the raw edge.

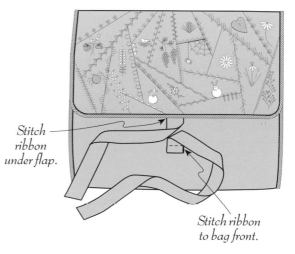

"Ladies were trained from birth to be decorative . . . to be appealingly helpless. . . . They were also trained to manage the intricate and demanding responsibilities of huge houses . . . while always making it seem that the house, the garden, the kitchen, and the servants ran themselves flawlessly while the lady of the house concentrated on matching colors of silk for her delicate embroidery."

—Alexandra Ripley, *Scarlett*, 1991

Evening Bag

Finished size: 5½" x 8"
Color photos on pages 35 and 42

MATERIALS

44"-WIDE FABRIC

¼ yd. stabilizer (lightweight interfacing)
or muslin for crazy-patch foundation

⅛ yd. each of 5 to 6 different fabrics for crazy patchwork

¼ yd. fabric for back of evening bag

¼ yd. fabric for lining

2½ yds. of ¼"-diameter decorative cording for finishing
and shoulder strap

¼ yd. decorative trim, such as 1"-wide trim or beads sewn
to seam-allowance tape, for bottom of bag (optional)

Assorted embroidery floss, perle cotton, and specialty cording

Silk ribbon, 2mm and 4mm, and ribbon floss

Metallic and invisible nylon thread (optional)

Assorted beads and buttons

Chenille, embroidery, tapestry, and beading needles

Clear tape

3" tassel (optional)

All measurements include ¼"-wide seam allowances.

CRAZY PATCHWORK

Before you begin, read "Crazy Patchwork" on pages 10–16 and choose a method. I recommend "Working from the Center" or "Pattern Piecing" for this project. Refer to the "Piecing and Embroidery Guide" on the pullout pattern.

1. From the stabilizer or muslin, cut a 6" x 8½" rectangle for the foundation of the crazy patchwork.

2. Cut and stitch pieces of the assorted fabrics to the foundation. Completely cover the foundation.

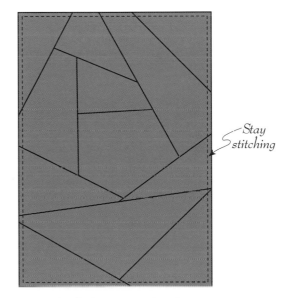

Stay stitching

Finished Crazy Patchwork

EMBROIDERY

Do not embroider into the seam allowance around the evening bag; this adds bulk and can make it difficult to construct the bag.

1. Embroider the crazy-patchwork seams. Refer to "Embroidery" on pages 17–32 and the pullout pattern for suggestions.

2. If desired, fill in the embroidery with beads. Use invisible nylon thread or embroidery floss in a similar color.

3. Place a terry-cloth towel on your pressing surface. Place the crazy patchwork, right side down, on the towel and press.

CONSTRUCTION

1. From backing fabric, cut a 6" x 8½" rectangle.

2. I used a decorative trim on the bottom of the black-and-red evening bag on page 42. If you have chosen a trim with a seam-allowance tape, stitch it to the right side of the backing fabric as shown. (A zipper foot will make stitching easier.)

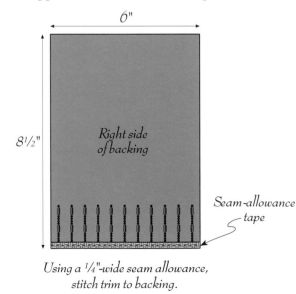

*Using a ¼"-wide seam allowance,
stitch trim to backing.*

3. Pin the front and back sides of the evening bag as shown, right sides together. Stitch down one side, across the bottom, and up the other side. Backstitch at the beginning and end. Remove pins. Turn to the right side and press.

*Stitch the sides and bottom
of the evening bag.*

4. From the lining fabric, cut two 6" x 8½" rectangles. Place the pieces right sides together. Stitch the long sides only and backstitch at the beginning and end. Trim the seam allowances to ⅛".

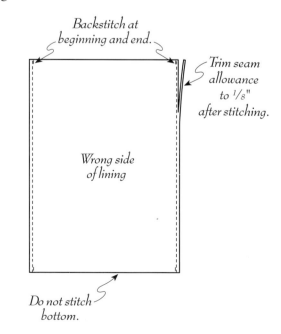

5. Place the bag sewn in step 3 inside the lining, right sides together. Match the evening bag and lining at the top and side seams. Stitch the top. Leave a ½"-wide opening at one side seam for the cording. If you plan to use different cording for trimming the bag and making the shoulder strap, leave a ½"-wide opening at both side seams.

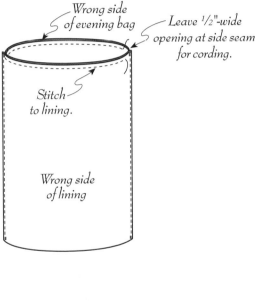

Wrong side of evening bag

Leave ½"-wide opening at side seam for cording.

Stitch to lining.

Wrong side of lining

6. Pull the lining right side out as shown. Turn the raw edges of the lining under ¼" and press. Hand or machine stitch ¹⁄₁₆" from the folded edge.

Turn ¼"-wide seam allowance under and stitch by hand or machine.

Right side of lining

7. Push the lining inside the evening bag. Press lightly at the top of the bag.

8. If you are using a decorative trim without a seam-allowance tape, hand stitch it to the bottom of the bag.

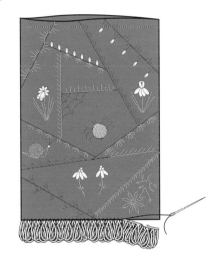

9. Tie a knot at one end of the cording, leaving a ¼"-long tail. Hand stitch the tail and knot at one top corner of the evening bag as shown.

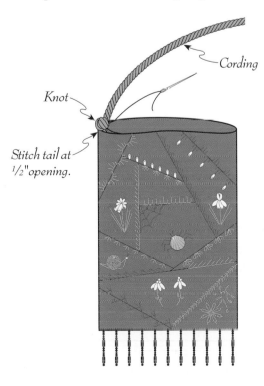

Cording

Knot

Stitch tail at ½" opening.

10. Hand stitch cording around the top of the evening bag. At the beginning knot, stitch cording to the knot. Continue stitching down the side, across the bottom front, and up the other side of the evening bag.

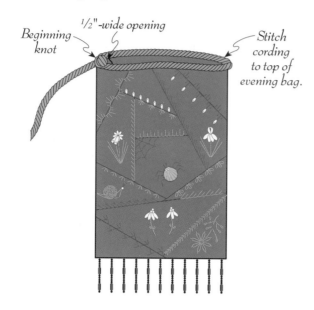

Beginning knot

½"-wide opening

Stitch cording to top of evening bag.

11. About 1" from the top of the evening bag, tie a knot to match the one at the beginning. Finish stitching so this knot is positioned at the opposite top corner as shown.

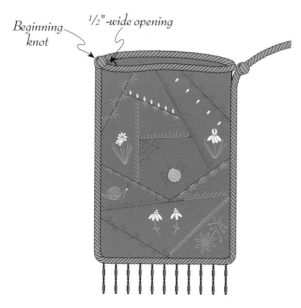

Beginning knot

½"-wide opening

12. Use the remaining cording to make the shoulder strap. Cut the cording to the desired length. (If desired, tie a knot every 3" before cutting.) To prevent raveling, wrap the end of the cording with clear tape before cutting. Push the end of the cording into the ½"-wide opening. Stitch the cording inside securely, then stitch the opening closed.

Stitch cording inside of ½"-wide opening.

13. If desired, stitch a 3" tassel to one top corner of the bag to finish.

Eyeglasses Case

Finished size: 3¾" x 7½"
Color photos on pages 35 and 43

MATERIALS

44"-WIDE FABRIC

¼ yd. stabilizer (medium-heavyweight interfacing) or muslin for crazy-patch foundation

⅛ yd. each of 5 to 6 different fabrics for crazy patchwork

¼ yd. fabric for back of eyeglasses case

¼ yd. fabric for lining

9" of ⅛"-diameter decorative cording for finishing

Assorted embroidery floss, perle cotton, and specialty cording

Silk ribbon, 2mm and 4mm, and ribbon floss

Metallic and invisible nylon thread (optional)

Assorted beads and buttons

Chenille, embroidery, tapestry, and beading needles

Clear tape

All measurements include ¼"-wide seam allowances.

CRAZY PATCHWORK

Before you begin, read "Crazy Patchwork" on pages 10–16 and choose a method. I recommend "Working from the Center" or "Pattern Piecing" for this project. Refer to the "Piecing and Embroidery Guide" on the pullout pattern. You will need to use a variation of the pattern-piecing method for this project. Stitch pieces 8a, 8b, and 8c together before stitching this unit to the foundation. Repeat for pieces 9a and 9b.

1. From the stabilizer or muslin, cut a 4¼" x 8" rectangle for the foundation of the crazy patchwork.

2. Cut and stitch pieces of the assorted fabrics to the foundation. Completely cover the foundation.

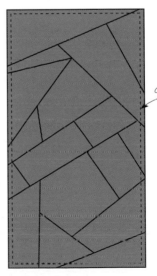

Stay stitching

Finished Crazy Patchwork

EMBROIDERY

Do not embroider into the seam allowance around the eyeglasses case; this adds bulk and can make it difficult to construct the case.

1. Embroider the crazy-patchwork seams. Refer to "Embroidery" on pages 17–32 and the pullout pattern for suggestions.

2. If desired, fill in the embroidery with beads. Use invisible nylon thread or embroidery floss in a similar color.

3. Place a terry-cloth towel on your pressing surface. Place the crazy patchwork, right side down, on the towel and press.

CONSTRUCTION

1. From the backing fabric, cut a 4¼" x 8" rectangle for the back of the eyeglasses case.

2. Pin the front and back sides of the eyeglasses case, right sides together. Stitch down one side, across the bottom, and up the other side. Backstitch at the beginning and end. Remove pins. Turn to the right side and press.

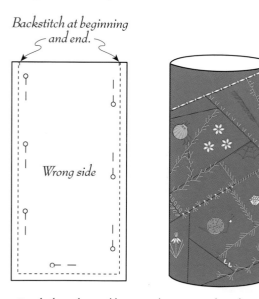

Stitch the sides and bottom, then turn right side out.

3. From the lining fabric, cut two 4¼" x 8" rectangles. Place the pieces right sides together. Stitch the long sides only, backstitching at the beginning and end. Trim the seam allowances to ⅛".

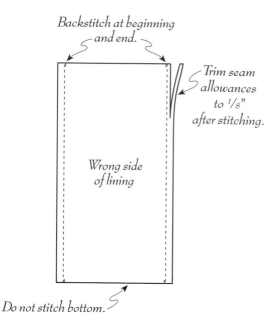

4. Place the case sewn in step 2 inside the lining, right sides together. Match the case and lining at the top and side seams. Stitch the top. Leave a ½"-wide opening at a side seam for the cording.

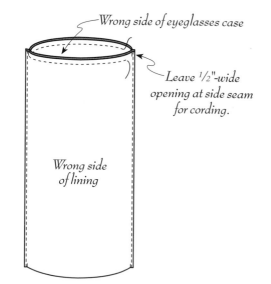

5. Pull the lining right side out. Turn the raw edges of the lining under ¼" and press. Hand or machine stitch ¹⁄₁₆" from the folded edge.

Turn ¼" seam allowance under and stitch by hand or machine.

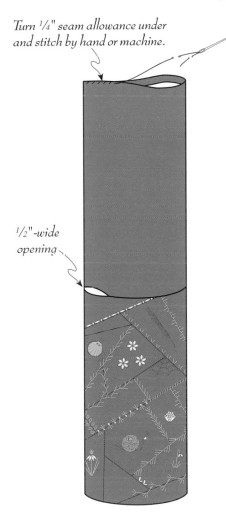

½"-wide opening

6. Push the lining inside the eyeglasses case. Press lightly at the top of the case.

7. Push one end of the cording into the ½"-wide opening. Hand stitch the cording inside securely, then stitch the cording around the top of the eyeglasses case as shown.

Stitch cording in ½"-wide opening.

8. When you have stitched around the top of the eyeglasses case, cut the excess cording, leaving a ½"-long tail. (To prevent raveling, tape the ends of the cording before cutting.) Push the end of the cording into the ½"-wide opening. Stitch the cording inside securely, then stitch the opening closed.

𝒯ᴵᴾ

You can also use a glue gun to attach the cording. Take care to use only a small amount of glue.

Scissors Case

Finished size: 2½" x 5½"
Color photo on page 35

MATERIALS

44"-WIDE FABRIC

¼ yd. stabilizer (medium-weight interfacing) or muslin
for crazy-patch foundation

⅛ yd. each of 4 to 5 different fabrics for crazy patchwork

⅛ yd. fabric for back of scissors case

¼ yd. fabric for lining

½ yd. of ⅛"-diameter decorative cording or
braid for finishing

Assorted embroidery floss, perle cotton, and specialty cording

Silk ribbon, 2mm and 4mm, and ribbon floss

Metallic and invisible nylon thread (optional)

Assorted beads and buttons

Chenille, embroidery, tapestry, and beading needles

Paper or template plastic

Clear tape

Snap

All measurements include ¼"-wide seam allowances.

CRAZY PATCHWORK

Before you begin, read "Crazy Patchwork" on pages 10–16 and choose a method. I recommend "Working from a Corner" or "Pattern Piecing" for this project. Refer to the "Piecing and Embroidery Guide" on the pullout pattern.

1. From the stabilizer or muslin, cut a 3" x 6" rectangle for the foundation of the crazy patchwork. Trace the pattern for the scissors case on the foundation.

2. Cut and stitch pieces of the assorted fabrics to the foundation. Completely cover the foundation.

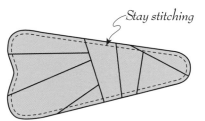

Finished Crazy Patchwork

EMBROIDERY

Do not embroider into the seam allowance around the scissors case; this adds bulk and can make it difficult to construct the case.

1. Embroider the crazy-patchwork seams. Refer to "Embroidery" on pages 17–32 and the pullout pattern for suggestions.

2. If desired, fill in the embroidery with beads. Use invisible nylon thread or embroidery floss in a similar color.

3. Place a terry-cloth towel on your pressing surface. Place the crazy patchwork, right side down, on the towel and press.

CONSTRUCTION

1. Referring to the pullout pattern, make a template for the scissors case by tracing the pattern on paper or template plastic.

2. Using the template, trace and cut 1 scissors-case pattern each from the remaining piece of foundation and backing fabric. Also, cut 2 pieces from the lining fabric.

3. Using an ⅛"-wide seam allowance, stitch the back of the scissors case to the foundation. Using foundation for the front and back of the scissors case helps protect your scissors.

4. Pin the front and back sides of the scissors case, right sides together. Using a ¼"-wide seam allowance, stitch around the case as shown. Backstitch at the beginning and end. Remove pins. Turn to the right side and press.

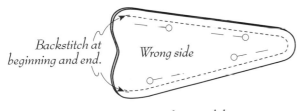

Backstitch at beginning and end. Wrong side

Stitch around the case.

5. Repeat step 4 for the lining of the scissors case, but trim the seam allowance to ⅛" after stitching.

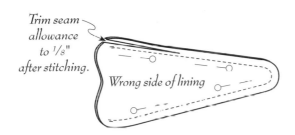

Trim seam allowance to ⅛" after stitching.

Wrong side of lining

6. Place the case sewn in step 4 inside the lining, *wrong* sides together. Turn the raw edges of the case and lining inside ¼" and baste. Hand stitch ¹⁄₁₆" from the folded edge, leaving a ½"-wide opening at both side seams.

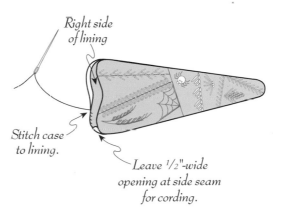

Right side of lining

Stitch case to lining.

Leave ½"-wide opening at side seam for cording.

7. Push one end of the decorative cording into one of the ½"-wide openings. Stitch the cording inside securely, then stitch the opening closed. Continue stitching cording around the sides and top as shown.

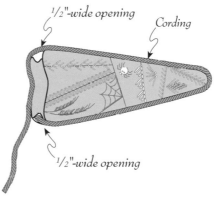

½"-wide opening   Cording

½"-wide opening

8. When you have stitched around the scissors case, cut the excess cording, leaving a ½"-long tail. (To prevent raveling, tape the ends of the cording before cutting.) Push the end of the cording into the remaining ½"-wide opening. Stitch the cording inside securely, then stitch the opening closed.

9. Finish by stitching a snap at the top center of the scissors case.

"I will honor Christmas in my heart and try
to keep it all the year."

—Charles Dickens, *A Christmas Carol*, 1843

Christmas Stocking

Finished size: 9½" x 15½"
Color photos on pages 40–41

MATERIALS

44"-WIDE FABRIC

⅜ yd. stabilizer (lightweight interfacing) or muslin for crazy-patch foundation

⅛ yd. each of 5 to 6 different fabrics for crazy patchwork

½ yd. fabric for back of stocking

½ yd. fabric for stocking lining

¼ yd. fabric for toe, heel, and cuff*

¼ yd. of ⅛"- to ¼"-diameter decorative cording for hanging loop

½ yd. of 1"-wide decorative trim for cuff

Assorted embroidery floss and perle cotton

Silk ribbon, 2mm and 4mm, and ribbon floss

Metallic and invisible nylon thread (optional)

Assorted beads and charms

Chenille, embroidery, tapestry, and beading needles

Paper or template plastic

*Use gold lamé for a glitzy look or corduroy for a Country or masculine look.

All measurements include ¼"-wide seam allowances.

CRAZY PATCHWORK

Before you begin, read "Crazy Patchwork" on pages 10–16 and choose a method. I recommend "Working from a Corner" or "Pattern Piecing" for this project. Refer to the "Piecing and Embroidery Guide" on the pullout pattern.

1. Trace the pattern for the stocking front on stabilizer or muslin as described for your chosen method, then cut out the stocking front. Use this as the foundation of the crazy patchwork.

2. Cut and stitch pieces of the assorted fabrics to the foundation. Completely cover the foundation. Pieces #1 and #16 are the toe and heel of the stocking.

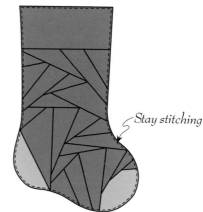

Stay stitching

Finished Crazy Patchwork

EMBROIDERY

Do not embroider into the seam allowances around the stocking. This adds bulk and can make it difficult to construct the stocking.

1. Embroider the crazy-patchwork seams. Refer to "Embroidery" on pages 17–32 and the pullout pattern for suggestions.

2. If desired, fill in the embroidery with beads. Use invisible nylon thread or embroidery floss in a similar color.

3. Place a terry-cloth towel on your pressing surface. Place the crazy patchwork, right side down, on the towel and press.

CONSTRUCTION

1. Referring to the pullout pattern, make a template for the stocking by tracing the pattern on paper or template plastic.

2. To make sure the stocking toe is pointed in the same direction as the crazy patchwork, place the template on the wrong side of the backing fabric. Trace and cut out the stocking back.

3. Place lining fabric right sides together. Using the template, trace and cut out the stocking.

4. With right sides together as shown, stitch the stocking front to the stocking back, backstitching at the beginning and end. Do not stitch across the top. Turn to the right side and gently press.

Stitch stocking front and back together.

TIP

LAMÉ

If you use lamé as in the pictured stocking (page 41), be very careful when pressing. Lamé can react badly to a hot iron! Use a pressing cloth.

5. With right sides together as shown, stitch the lining front to the lining back. Leave a 5"-wide opening between the **X**s. Do not stitch across the top.

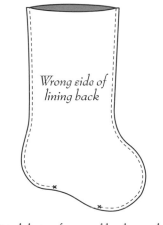

Stitch lining front and back together. Leave a 5"-wide opening.

6. To make the stocking cuff, cut 2 rectangles, each 4" x 14½", from the cuff fabric. Stitch decorative cording to a long side of 1 rectangle. (This will be the cuff. The other piece will be the cuff lining.) With right sides facing as shown, stitch the short ends of the cuff together. Repeat for the cuff lining.

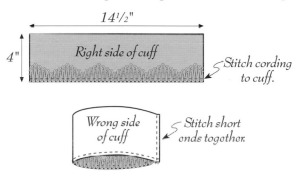

14½"
4"
Right side of cuff
Stitch cording to cuff.

Wrong side of cuff
Stitch short ends together.

7. Place the cuff lining inside the cuff. Stitch over the cording as shown. Turn the cuff to the right side and press gently.

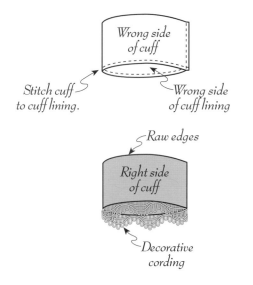

8. Place the cuff over the stocking, with the wrong side of the cuff to the right side of the stocking. Align the cuff seam and stocking seam as shown. Baste the cuff to the stocking.

9. Cut a 6"-long piece of cording for the hanging loop. Fold in half and align the ends of the cording with the raw edge of the stocking. Stitch.

10. Place the stocking inside the lining, right sides together. Align the raw edges and the seams on the left side. Stitch.

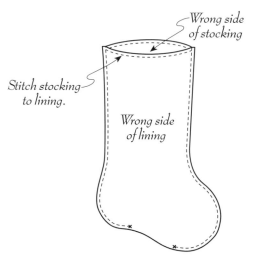

11. Gently pull the stocking through the opening in the lining. Fold the raw edges of the opening inside ¼" and stitch. Push the lining into the stocking.

12. Pull cuff away from the stocking and topstitch the stocking to the lining, ⅛" below the cuff seam. This will prevent the lining from rolling out of the stocking top. Fold the cuff over the stocking.

Christmas Ornament

Finished size: 3½" x 3½"

Color photos on pages 40–41

MATERIALS

44"-WIDE FABRIC

¼ yd. stabilizer (lightweight interfacing) or muslin for crazy-patch foundation

⅛ yd. each of 4 to 5 different fabrics for crazy patchwork

¼ yd. thin batting, such as Hobbs Thermore®

¾ yd. of ⅛"-diameter decorative cording for finishing

Assorted embroidery floss, perle cotton, and specialty cording

Silk ribbon, 2mm and 4mm, and ribbon floss

Metallic and invisible nylon thread (optional)

Assorted beads and buttons

Chenille, embroidery, tapestry, and beading needles

Paper or template plastic

Medium-weight art board

Spray adhesive

Glue gun (optional)

Clear tape

3" tassel (optional)

All measurements include ¼"-wide seam allowances.

CRAZY PATCHWORK

Before you begin, read "Crazy Patchwork" on pages 10–16 and choose a method. I recommend "Working from the Center" or "Pattern Piecing" for this project. Refer to the "Piecing and Embroidery Guide" on the pullout pattern.

1. From stabilizer or muslin, cut a 4½" x 4½" square for the foundation of the crazy patchwork.

2. Cut and stitch pieces of the assorted fabrics to the foundation. Completely cover the foundation.

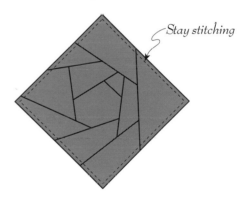

Stay stitching

EMBROIDERY

Do not embroider into the turn-under allowances around the ornament. This adds bulk and can make it difficult to construct the ornament.

1. Embroider the crazy-patchwork seams. Refer to "Embroidery" on pages 17–32 and the pullout pattern for suggestions.

2. If desired, fill in the embroidery with beads. Use invisible nylon thread or embroidery floss in a similar color.

3. Place a terry-cloth towel on your pressing surface. Place the crazy patchwork, right side down, on the towel and press.

CONSTRUCTION

1. Referring to the pullout pattern, make a template for the ornament by tracing the pattern on paper or template plastic.

2. From the medium-weight art board, cut a 3½" x 3½" square.

3. From the batting, cut a 4" x 4" square.

4. Using spray adhesive or a glue gun, attach the batting to the art board. Wrap the batting around to the back side of the art board and glue. Trim excess batting at the corners.

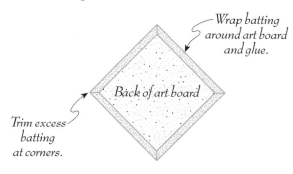

Wrap batting around art board and glue.

Back of art board

Trim excess batting at corners.

5. Spray the batting with a small amount of adhesive. Place the crazy patchwork, right side up, on the batting. Wrap the crazy patchwork around to the back side of the art board and glue. Clip the turn-over allowance where necessary.

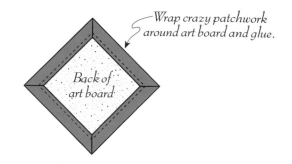

Wrap crazy patchwork around art board and glue.

Back of art board

6. Using the template prepared in step 1, cut fabric to cover the ornament back. Fold under the ¼"-wide seam allowance and press.

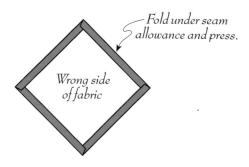

Fold under seam allowance and press.

Wrong side of fabric

7. Glue the backing fabric to the back side of the art board as shown.

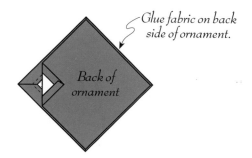

Glue fabric on back side of ornament.

Back of ornament

8. Lay the ornament on point as shown. Leaving a 6"-long tail, glue the cording around the edges of the ornament. Tie the cording in a knot at the top of the ornament. To prevent raveling, wrap the end of the cording with clear tape before cutting. Trim the excess cording to 6".

9. To finish, tie the cording tails in another knot as shown. Pull the knot tightly, then trim the tails. Stitch or glue a tassel to the bottom of the ornament if desired.

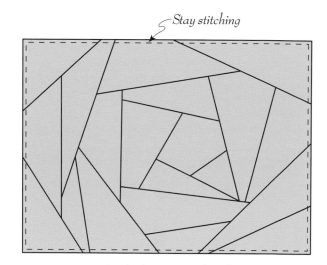
Book Cover

Finished size: 7¾" x 10½" (Standard paperback book)
Color photos on pages 35 and 38–39

MATERIALS

44"-WIDE FABRIC

⅜ yd. stabilizer (lightweight interfacing) or muslin for
crazy-patch foundation

⅛ yd. each of 5 to 6 different fabrics for crazy patchwork

¼ yd. fabric for lining and book flaps

1⅛ yds. of ⅛"-diameter decorative cording with
¼"-wide seam-allowance tape

¼ yd. of ¼"- to ½"-wide ribbon for bookmark (optional)

Assorted embroidery floss, perle cotton, and specialty cording

Silk ribbon, 2mm and 4mm, and ribbon floss

Metallic and invisible nylon thread (optional)

Assorted beads and buttons

Chenille, embroidery, tapestry, and beading needles

Paper or template plastic

All measurements include ¼"-wide seam allowances.

CRAZY PATCHWORK

Before you begin, read "Crazy Patchwork" on pages 10–16 and choose a crazy-patch method. I recommend "Working from the Center" or "Pattern Piecing" for this project. Refer to "Piecing and Embroidery Guide" on the pullout pattern.

1. From the stabilizer or muslin, cut a 8¼" x 11¼" rectangle for the foundation of the crazy patchwork.

2. Cut and stitch pieces of the assorted fabrics to the foundation. Completely cover the foundation.

Stay stitching

Finished Crazy Patchwork

EMBROIDERY

Do not embroider into the seam allowances around the book cover. This adds bulk and can make it difficult to construct the cover.

1. Embroider the crazy-patchwork seams. Refer to "Embroidery" on pages 17–32 and the pullout pattern for suggestions.

2. If desired, fill in the embroidery with beads. Use invisible nylon thread or embroidery floss in a similar color.

3. Place a terry-cloth towel on your pressing surface. Place the crazy patchwork, right side down, on the towel and press.

CONSTRUCTION

1. From the fabric for lining and book flaps, cut one 8¼" x 11¼" rectangle for the lining and two 4" x 8¼" rectangles for the book flaps.

2. Turn under a long side of each book flap ¼" as shown and stitch.

Turn under and stitch.

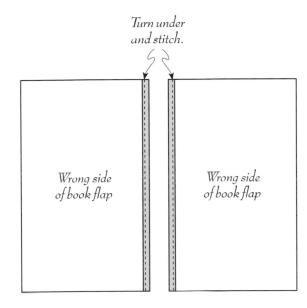

Wrong side of book flap

Wrong side of book flap

3. To include a bookmark, cut an 8"-long piece of the ¼"- to ½"-wide ribbon. Mark the center of the top long side of the crazy patchwork rectangle. Pin the ribbon at the center mark on the right side of the rectangle, aligning one end of the ribbon with the raw edge of the patchwork. Using a ¼"-wide seam allowance, stitch the ribbon in place. Pin the ribbon to the crazy patchwork until you have stitched the book cover together (so you won't catch the ribbon in another seam).

4. Stitch the decorative cording around the outside of the crazy patchwork rectangle as shown. Overlap the beginning and end of the cording in the seam allowance.

Clip seam-allowance tape at corners.

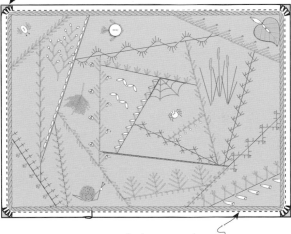

Stitch close to cording.

71

5. Place the book flaps on the crazy patchwork, right sides together, as shown. Align the outside edges and baste.

6. Place the lining on top of the crazy patchwork and book flaps, right sides together. Stitch as shown. Leave a 3"-wide opening for turning the book cover. Backstitch at the beginning and end of the stitching.

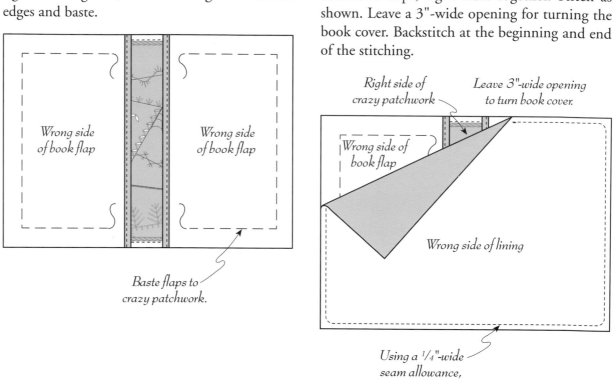

Wrong side of book flap

Wrong side of book flap

Baste flaps to crazy patchwork.

Right side of crazy patchwork

Leave 3"-wide opening to turn book cover.

Wrong side of book flap

Wrong side of lining

Using a ¹⁄₄"-wide seam allowance, stitch crazy patchwork, book flaps, and lining.

7. Turn the book cover right side out and press gently. Hand stitch the opening closed.

"This work is but canvas to our imagination."

—Henry David Thoreau (1817–62)

Footstool Cover

Finished size: For a 10½" x 12½" footstool
Color photos on pages 33 and 44

MATERIALS

44"-WIDE FABRIC

½ yd. stabilizer (lightweight interfacing) or muslin for crazy-patch foundation (See tip below.)

⅛ yd. each of 5 to 6 different fabrics for crazy patchwork

Assorted embroidery floss, perle cotton, and specialty cording

Silk ribbon, 2mm and 4mm, and ribbon floss

Metallic and invisible nylon thread (optional)

Assorted beads and buttons

Chenille, embroidery, tapestry, and beading needles

Staple gun

All measurements include ¼"-wide seam allowances.

CRAZY PATCHWORK

Before you begin, read "Crazy Patchwork" on pages 10–16 and choose a crazy-patch method. I recommend "Working from a Corner" or "Pattern Piecing" for this project. Refer to the "Piecing and Embroidery Guide" on the pullout pattern.

1. From the stabilizer or muslin, cut a 14" x 16" rectangle for the foundation of the crazy patchwork.

2. Cut and stitch pieces of the assorted fabrics to the foundation. You can use larger pieces around the outside edge because the 1½"-wide seam allowance will be turned under.

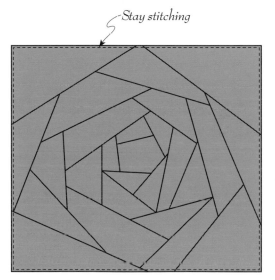

Finished Crazy Patchwork

ℐIP

FOR DIFFERENT SIZES

If you want to cover a different size footstool or chair seat, measure the top and cut a piece of foundation 1½" larger all around than the stool or chair seat. For example, if your chair seat is 12" x 16", cut a 15" x 19" rectangle from the foundation.

EMBROIDERY

Do not embroider into the seam allowances around the footstool cover. This adds bulk and can make it difficult to construct the cover.

1. Embroider the crazy-patchwork seams. Refer to "Embroidery" on pages 17–32 and the pullout pattern for suggestions.

2. If desired, fill in the embroidery with beads. Use invisible nylon thread or embroidery floss in a similar color.

3. Place a terry-cloth towel on your pressing surface. Place the crazy patchwork, right side down, on the towel and press.

CONSTRUCTION

1. Remove the footstool cover or chair seat from the frame. (Turn the footstool or chair upside down and remove the long screws at each corner.)

2. Place the crazy patchwork on the footstool cover or chair seat. Pull the edges to the back side.

Pulling tightly, staple the corners, the middle of each side, and every 1" to 1½". Trim the excess at the corners.

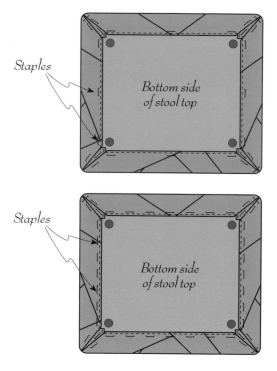

Staples

Bottom side of stool top

Staples

Bottom side of stool top

3. Return the footstool cover or chair seat to the frame and replace the screws.

TIP

ADDING BATTING TO AN OLD FOOTSTOOL

If your footstool or chair is older, consider adding a layer of thin batting. The extra volume enhances the appearance of the finished project. Cut a piece of batting 1" larger than the stool top all around. Place the batting on the footstool cover or chair seat, pulling the excess to the back side. Pull the batting tight and staple. Trim the excess batting at the corners.

Staple batting.

Padding on stool top covered with batting

> *"Some books are to be tasted, others to be swallowed, and some few to be chewed and digested...."*
>
> —Francis Bacon (1561–1626)

Bibliography

SOURCES

Applegarth, Margaret T., ed., *Heirlooms.* New York: Harper and Row, 1967.

Ferber, Edna. *Giant.* New York: Doubleday and Company, 1952.

Linton, George, comp., *A Dictionary of Textile Terms by Dan River.* New York: Dan River, 1980.

Maggio, Rosalie, ed., *Quotations by Women.* Boston: Beacon Press, 1992.

Mosey, Caron L. *America's Pictorial Quilts.* Paducah, Ky.: American Quilter's Society, 1985.

Randall, Esther. *Embellishing with Silk Ribbon Embroidery.* Cumming, Iowa: Landauer Books, 1996.

Ripley, Alexandra. *Scarlett.* New York: Warner Books, 1991.

Webster, Marie D. *Quilts—Their Story and How to Make Them.* New York: Doubleday, Page and Company, 1915.

SUGGESTED READING

APPLIQUÉ

Linker, Sue. *Sunbonnet Sue All Through the Year.* Bothell, Wash.: That Patchwork Place, 1994.

EMBROIDERY

Heazlewood, Merrilyn. *Spring Bulb Sampler.* Tasmania, Australia: Little Stitches, 1991.

———. *Cottage Garden.* Tasmania, Australia: Merriwood Press, 1994.

Montano, Judith Baker. *Crazy Quilt Odyssey.* Lafayette, Calif.: C & T Publishing, 1991.

———. *Elegant Stitches.* Lafayette, Calif.: C & T Publishing, 1995.

Webster, Marie D. *Quilts—Their Story and How to Make Them.* New York: Doubleday, Page and Company, 1915.

West, Deanna Hall. *An Encyclopedia of Ribbon Embroidery Flowers.* San Marcos, Calif.: American School of Needlework, Inc., 1995.

QUILTMAKING

Kimball, Jeana. *Loving Stitches.* Bothell, Wash.: That Patchwork Place, 1992.

Leone, Diane. *Fine Hand Quilting.* Mountain View, Calif.: Leone Publications, 1986.

Resources

NEEDLE-ARTS SUPPLIES
IN THE UNITED STATES

The Children's Corner
3814 Cleghorn Avenue
Nashville, TN 37215
1-800-543-6915

Metamorphosis
2176 Bandywood Drive
Nashville, TN 37215
1-800-341-4203

Nordic Needle
1314 Gateway Drive
Fargo, ND 58103
1-800-433-4321

FURNITURE FOR NEEDLE
ARTS IN THE UNITED STATES

Freeman and Company
PO Box 362
Thomasville, NC 27361-0362
1-910-476-6215
1-910-476-4936

NEEDLE-ARTS SUPPLIES
IN AUSTRALIA, CANADA,
ENGLAND, AND NEW ZEALAND

The Calico House
2 Napoleon Street
Cottesloe 6011
Western Australia

Chattels
53 Chalk Farm Road
London, England NW1 8AN
071-267-0877

Down Under Designs
#3559 Sydney Road
Seaforth, NSW 0292
Australia
02-948-5575

Margaret Barret Distributors Ltd.
19 Beasley Avenue
PO Box 12-034
Penrose, Auckland
New Zealand
64-9-525-6142

Needle Art
72 Valleyford Avenue
Richmond Hill, Ontario L4C OA6
Canada
905-770-5368

Needlecraft International Pty. Ltd.
96 Rowe Street
Eastwood, NSW 2122
Australia
008-263-977 (toll free) or 02-858-2815

The Stitch Shop
15 The Podium
Bath Avon, England BA1 5AL

About the Author

*L*ezette Thomason is co-owner of The Children's Corner, a retail and wholesale company for heirloom sewing supplies, where she has been a teacher and designer for eighteen years. She also teaches twice yearly at the Martha Pullen School of Sewing in Huntsville, Alabama. Beginning in 1997, Lezette will teach for Needlecraft International in Sydney, Australia, at "Sewing in the Blue Mountains." She lives in Nashville, Tennessee, with her husband, Michael, and their cat, Sock. Lezette has a grown daughter, Anne.

Index

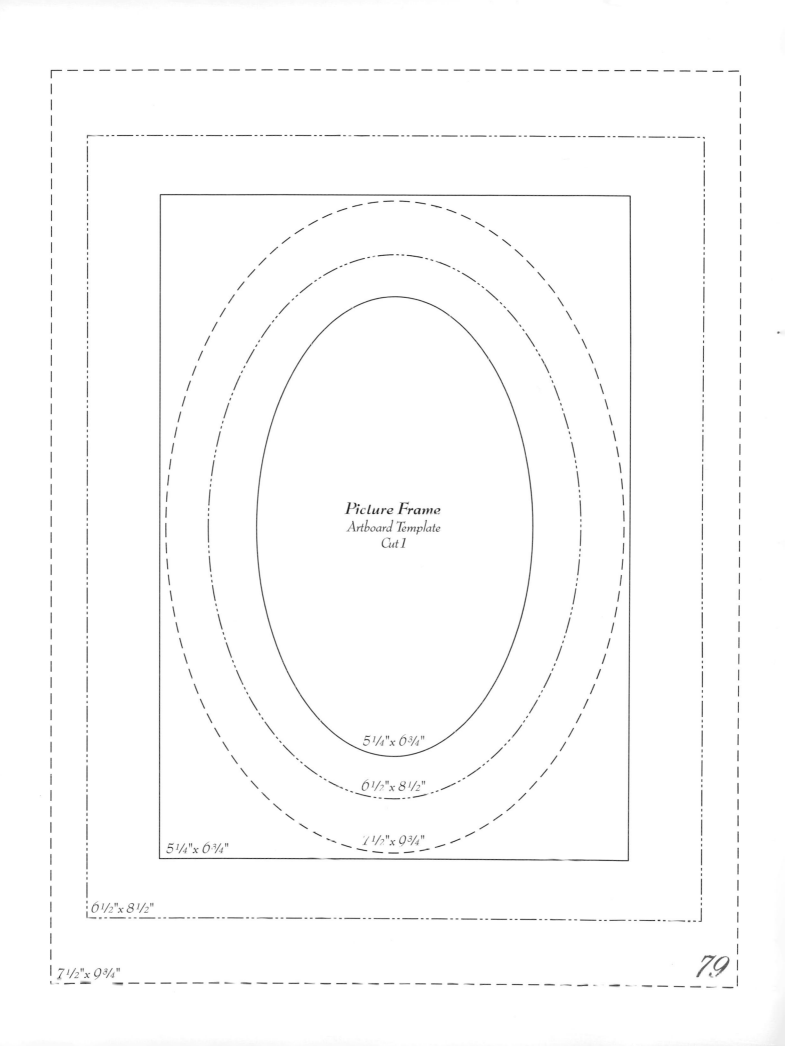

Picture Frame
Artboard Template
Cut 1

5¼"x 6¾"

6½"x 8½"

7½"x 9¾"

5¼"x 6¾"

6½"x 8½"

7½"x 9¾"

79

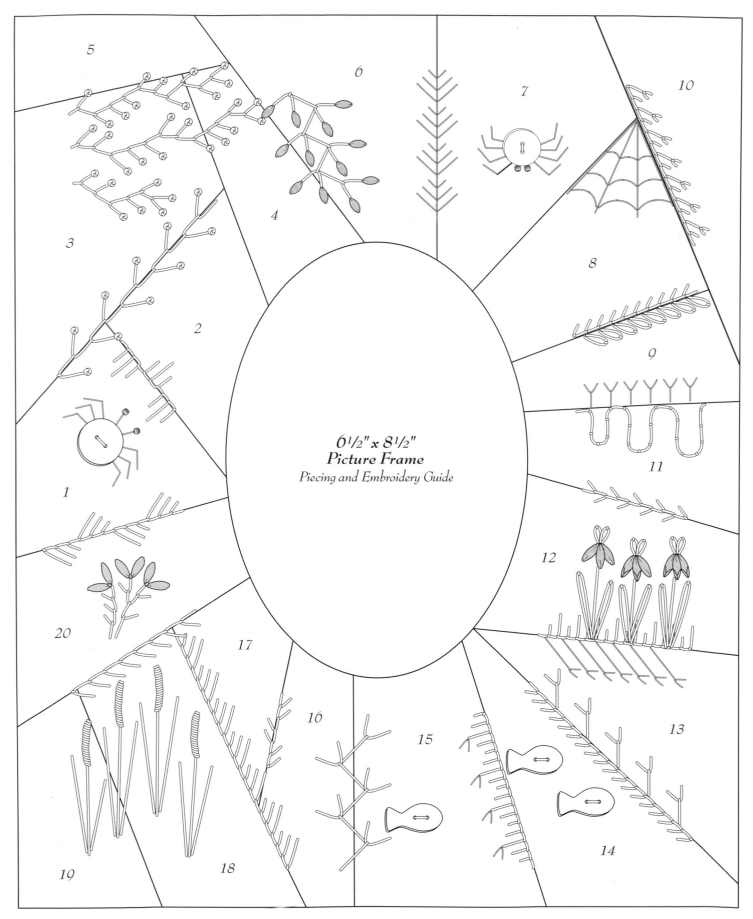

6½" x 8½"
Picture Frame
Piecing and Embroidery Guide

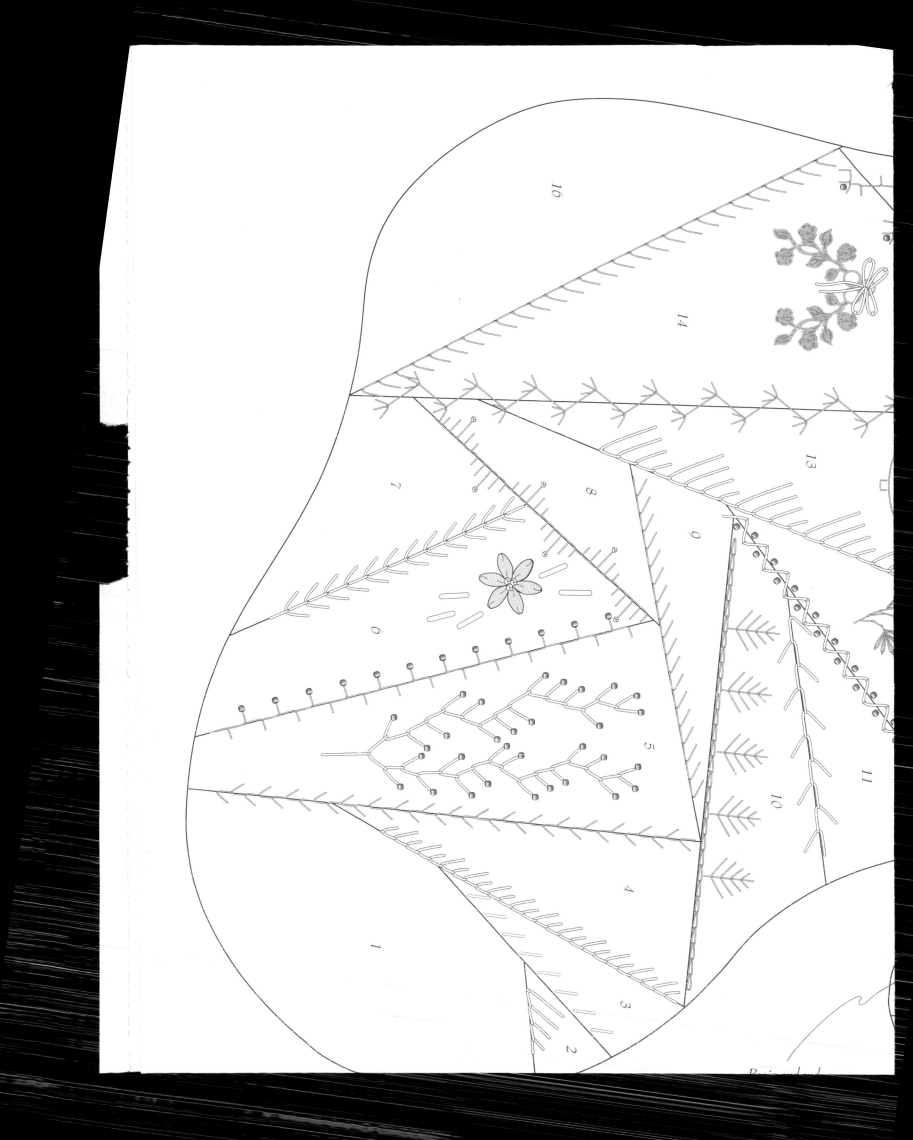

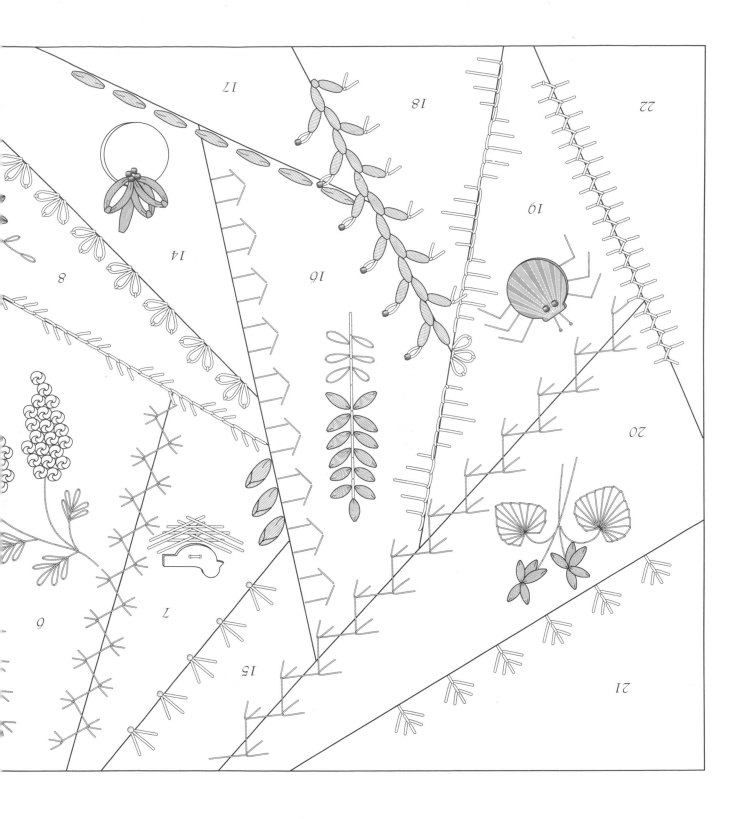